New Directions in Development

Other Titles in This Series

Getting It Off the Shelf: A Methodology for Implementing Federal Research, Peter W. House and David W. Jones, Jr.

Alternatives for Delivering Public Services: Toward Improved Performance, edited by E. S. Savas

Inside the Bureaucracy: The View from the Assistant Secretary's Desk, Thomas Murphy, Donald Nuechterlein, and Ronald J. Stupak

Life Cycle Costing: A Better Method of Government Procurement, Robert M. Seldon

Technology Transfer to Cities: Processes of Choice at the Local Level, W. Henry Lambright

The President, the Budget, and Congress, James P. Pfiffner

Westview Special Studies in Public Policy and Public Systems Management

New Directions in Development: A Study of U.S. AID
Donald R. Mickelwait, Charles F. Sweet, and Elliott R. Morss

In 1973 Congress legislated a fundamental change in U.S. foreign aid policy: rather than provide general assistance to developing nations, the U.S. Agency for International Development (AID) would focus on helping the rural poor in those nations. AID commissioned Development Alternatives, Inc. (DAI), to prepare a strategy for making the change toward "New Directions" in development and then to assist in the design and implementation of a number of projects using the new strategy.

The authors describe the bureaucratic and administrative problems that confronted Development Alternatives in this job, giving particular attention to the administrative and bureaucratic barriers within AID itself. They conclude with a set of recommendations for reform that are essential if the agency is to attain its "New Directions" objectives.

Donald R. Mickelwait, president of DAI, is currently designing information systems to support rural development projects.

Charles F. Sweet, vice-president of DAI, directs a study of local private organizations in the rural areas of developing nations.

Elliott R. Morss, director of research at DAI, is studying bureaucratic behavior and other constraints that impede the development effectiveness of bilateral and multilateral efforts.

New Directions in Development: A Study of U.S. AID

Donald R. Mickelwait, Charles F. Sweet, and Elliott R. Morss

Routledge
Taylor & Francis Group
LONDON AND NEW YORK

First published 1979 by Westview Press

Published 2018 by Routledge
52 Vanderbilt Avenue, New York, NY 10017
2 Park Square, Milton Park, Abingdon, Oxon OX14 4RN

Routledge is an imprint of the Taylor & Francis Group, an informa business

Library of Congress Catalog Card Number: 79-5059

ISBN 13: 978-0-367-01790-3(hbk)
ISBN 13: 978-0-367-16777-6(pbk)

Contents

SECTION II
REFLECTIONS ON THE PROCESS APPROACH
TO PROJECT DEVELOPMENT

Tables and Figures

Table

Figure

Preface

In 1973 the Agency for International Development (AID) asked Development Alternatives, Inc. (DAI), to assist in the development of project strategies to attain the goals of the "New Directions" Congressional mandate to focus assistance on the rural poor. With the completion of this work, late in 1975, AID asked DAI to assist in the design of twelve rural development projects in ten countries which, taken together, are budgeted at $65 million.

This report describes the design efforts themselves, documents the frequently tortuous process of moving the projects through the AID review and approval system, and discusses the problems of implementation that follow.

At this writing, about half the projects have only recently reached the implementation stage. Thus it is too early to say which design efforts or which design and implementation approach resulted in the greatest benefit to the rural poor in the the countries involved. Nonetheless, the design efforts themselves, coupled with a tracing of the projects as they moved through the review and approval process, have uncovered serious constraints in AID's present procedures, which hinder the pursuit of the "New Directions" mandate. This report documents these deficiencies and presents recommendations to overcome them.

This report is but one of a large number of studies and assessments completed by DAI on development assistance, shown in Annex B. This knowledge base is used to extend the conclusions beyond the immediate sample of twelve to a broad experience with AID approaches and policies.

This work is the product of considerable effort of several of the DAI staff, as well as the authors.

Charles F. Sweet was the principal DAI project designer in Africa, and contributed the material for Chapters 2 and 6. Elliott R. Morss directed the Washington-based tracing of project histories and, aided by Victoria Sorsby, conducted interviews and developed content analyses. He is largely responsible for Chapter 3 and the quantitative analysis in Chapter 5, as well as Chapter 9. In addition, as Director of Research, he reviewed all material submitted by other authors.

Donald R. Mickelwait oversaw design efforts in Latin America and Afghanistan, provided the original material for Chapters 1 and 4 and the qualitative portion of Chapter 5. He served as the overall coordinator for the Project. The work also benefits greatly from the efforts of Tony Barclay, who provided the original material for Chapter 7, and Craig Olson, who was the primary author of Chapter 8, with assistance from Robert Rich of Princeton University, and George Honadle of DAI.

These people are merely the front-runners in what has been a group effort. DAI utilizes a team approach, and nine unmentioned staff worked in the field to capture the essence of local dynamics in our assigned areas. Likewise this report profits from reviews, editing and discussions by non-authors, which often substantially changed and improved the original contribution. James Woldahl has typed uncounted drafts of this report, and has faithfully seen it through to its present form. Billie Jo Williams has served as editor and production manager.

Dr. Alice Morton has most recently been the project monitor, and furnished valuable recommendations on the draft report. Apart from her office, only the Office of Technical Support of the Near East Bureau was able to provide comments on the October 1977 draft, which were greatly appreciated. In addition to catching inadvertent errors, such reviews proved valuable in pointing up the multiplicity of explanations that can be used for the same objective facts.

The study reappeared in January 1978, and underwent a lengthy review process in the Agency for International Development. The current version reflects and has benefited from a series of meetings between the authors and staff in AID/Washington. Information on the projects studied is current through October 1977, but updated in selected instances through June 1978.

At the urging of readers of the draft, we have sharpened the analysis, attributed more specific causes to the effects noted, and drawn more conclusions and recommendations. We believe the potential knowledge gained from such an exercise is a positive contribution to AID and the development community. We appreciate the efforts of those who contributed to this study, and hope the insights will be reflected in the next generation of "New Directions" development assistance projects.

Donald R. Mickelwait
Charles F. Sweet
Elliott R. Morss

Washington, D.C.
March 1979

Prologue

In January 1979, after long and heated internal controversy, the Agency for International Development delegated considerable project approval authority to the field. Missions now have the authority to approve projects having a total value of up to five million dollars for the life of the project, and Regional Assistant Administrators may delegate further authority to Missions to approve projects up to a maximum of ten million dollars. Furthermore, while preliminary project documents (PIDs) must still be reviewed in Washington, this review must be completed within thirty days.

This delegation of approval authority for projects was a hard-fought and critical step in the rationalization of AID's project identification, review and approval process. Administrator Gilligan has stated:[1]

> We have had several studies of the process for identifying, reviewing and approving field projects. Each study has made a persuasive case that both the efficiency and the effectiveness of the Agency would be improved by delegating greater authority to the field missions where the principal work is conducted.

This study is one of those to which Gilligan was referring, and argues that the delegation of project approval authority and project accountability to field missions is an essential procedural reform if AID is to fulfill on its responsibility to attempt to implement the "New Directions" mandate. When it appeared in January 1978, it aroused vigorous criticism from those in AID who believed AID/Washington should monitor mission activities closely to ensure compliance with Congressional directives. The change in policy reflects efforts of insiders, which were supported by empirical evidence, such as that presented here, that the old bureaucratic system was at odds with its own objectives.

The delegation to the field of authority to commit development assistance money is a necessary first step in the improvement of AID's procedures, if there is going to be meaningful development in the Third and Fourth Worlds. A second essential step is argued for here. The delegation of approval authority should be accompanied by a move to make field missions accountable for project results. In short, missions should be responsible for the projects they initiate. Accountability is only meaningful when there is a capacity to assess project impact. To ensure objectivity, it is essential that this evaluation capability reside in an independent office at headquarters.

There is considerable Congressional interest in such reforms. Section 125 of the International Development Assistance Act of 1978 (the Glenn Amendment)[2] directs the Administrator to improve the assessment and evaluation of programs and projects, to consult with Congress in establishing standards for such evaluations, and to report on these efforts annually. It remains to be seen how the Agency will go about responding to this legislation.

NOTES

[1] John J. Gilligan, Memorandum for the Executive Staff, Agency for International Development, December 20, 1978.

[2] "Report of the Committee on Foreign Relations, United States Senate, Together with Additional Views on S.3074," 95th Congress, Second Session, Report No. 95-840, U.S. Government Printing Office, Washington, D.C., 1978, pp. 30-31.

New Directions in Development

Introduction

This report discusses recent DAI work assisting in the design of development projects intended to benefit the rural poor. Definitive judgments on the impact of this work must await full implementation of the projects, but the opportunity exists now to draw lessons from the experience with project conceptualization, planning, and design over a period of several years.

ORIGINS OF THE "NEW DIRECTIONS" MANDATE

Awareness of the need to concentrate development efforts on small farmers has been growing during the past decade. Until the late 1960s, foreign donors placed priority on helping to maximize the rate of increase in the aggregate agricultural output and income of Third World countries. Since that time, attention has been shifting to a specific focus on the rural poor, with strong emphasis being given to the promotion of equity in the development process. It has become increasingly apparent that, in many cases, the applications of advances in agricultural technology, such as those associated with the Green Revolution, were increasing both absolute and relative income disparities among farmers in developing countries.[1]

The new focus was manifested in policy directives that were issued almost simultaneously within the World Bank and the Agency for International Development (AID). Robert McNamara, addressing the Board of Governors of the World Bank in 1973, said:

> The fact is that very little has been done over the past two decades specifically designed to increase the productivity of

> subsistence agriculture. Neither political programs, nor economic plans, nor international assistance -- bilateral or multilateral -- have given the problem serious and sustained attention. The World Bank is no exception. In our more than a quarter century of operations, less than $1 billion out of our $25 billion of lending has been devoted directly to this problem.
>
> It is time for all of us to confront this issue head-on.
>
> I suggest that the goal be to increase production on small farms so that by 1985 their output will be growing at the rate of 5% per year. If the goal is met, and smallholders maintain that momentum, they can double their annual output between 1985 and the end of the century.[2]

Congress expressed similar concerns in 1973 amendments to the Foreign Assistance Act:

> United States bilateral development assistance should give the highest priority to undertakings submitted by host governments which directly improve the lives of the poorest of their people and their capacity to participate in the development of their countries.[3]

It should be noted that this change in emphasis constituted a radical departure from earlier development priorities. In the past foreign donor priorities were placed on increasing the pace of overall economic development; the new thrust is to target development assistance on helping the poor of developing nations. It is relevant to note here that this change in emphasis was greater than that of the U.S. "war on poverty," which was attempted domestically in the 1960s. The enabling legislation did not subordinate the mandate for growth of the Employment Act of 1946 to equity considerations; it simply added the "war on poverty" to it. In contrast, it appears that McNamara and the Congress wanted a more extreme change in emphasis: The distributional objective was to assume primary importance.

Beyond calling for a change in emphasis, Congress specified in some detail how this was to be accomplished:

> ...greatest emphasis shall be placed on countries and activities which effectively involve the poor in development, by expanding their access to the economy through services and institutions at the local level, increasing labor-intensive production, spreading productive investment and services out from major cities to small towns and outlying rural areas, and otherwise providing opportunities for the poor to better their lives through their own effort.
>
> Bilateral development aid should concentrate increasingly on sharing American technical expertise, farm commodities, and industrial goods to meet critical development problems, and less on large-scale capital transfers....

While specification of implementation guidelines might be pleasing to certain observers of Congress,[4] such detailed instructions could prove to be excessively limiting. In short, Congress might have allowed AID at least some time to find appropriate information modes prior to imposing its own narrow implementation strictures on the Agency.[5]

The question of whether Congress went further than appropriate in specifying how the New Directions mandate should be implemented is not the focal point of this study. But it is important to recognize the significance of the change in policy focus and the attendant problems of finding ways to implement it. Four years after the issuance of the New Directions mandate two fundamental questions remain unresolved:

- How can development projects be structured so as to implement the general prescription that the rural poor must be involved in and benefit from foreign assistance? and

- How can AID, or other large foreign donors, be organized and managed to promote the necessary design and implementation of development projects that comply with the New Directions mandate?

Against this backdrop of uncertainty, AID has taken several initiatives to explore ways and means of translating the new policy focus into effective action. This report describes one of the methods that has evolved, where particular attention was given to stimulating local action by small farmers themselves, with a view to generating self-sustaining development activities.

ONE AID RESPONSE TO THE MANDATE

On July 12, 1973, the Technical Assistance Bureau (TAB) of AID entered into a contractual agreement with Development Alternatives, Inc. (DAI), to:

> Assist the Office of Development Administration, TAB, and overseas missions and local collaborators specified by TAB to identify ways of improving the design and execution of development assistance programs and projects whose success depends on individual or group action by low-income segments of rural populations in LDCs.
>
> The Contractor shall carry out a program of data development and analysis to:
>
> (i) Identify important linkages and general conditions leading to effective local action within rural development programs;
>
> (ii) Specify and elaborate quantitative and behavioral models, construct and test hypotheses in the field of local action capabilities; and
>
> (iii) Provide consulting assistance to field missions and local collaborating entities, aimed at improving their ability to collect, analyze and utilize local data to improve the effectiveness of rural development programs and projects which they are carrying out or providing support to.[6]

This work, which entailed a comparative analysis of 36 rural development projects in Africa (22) and Latin America (14), was completed in May 1975. The report was widely distributed within AID/Washington and was sent to every overseas AID Mission.[7] In the present volume that document will be referred to as the *Strategies* report.

On the basis of its findings, DAI recommended that projects intended to assist small farmers should be developed within the framework of a "process approach." This framework diverged sharply from conventional procedures where the project design is meant to function as a blueprint for every significant activity, with inputs and outputs specified in advance, and in great detail. The conventional approach assumes that solutions to the problems of the rural poor are known, and that projects are vehicles for applying them.

Since the process approach is often contrasted with alternative methods of planning development projects, which carried the day in some of the 12 projects studied, summary characterizations are valuable for this volume's discussions. Since the emphasis of the conventional approach is on upfront planning and highly specific and detailed mapping and schedules prior to the beginning of implementation, it is referred to as the "blueprint" approach. This produces projects designed to:

- Transfer known technology through a detailed plan generated prior to the active initiation of the project;

- Develop institutions and provide technical assistance above the grass-roots level;

- Spend funds in a prescribed and well-defined manner; and

- Generate income greater than project expenses as determined on the basis of paper exercises prior to project start-up.

When the goal is to hurry a project into implementation with a splash of foreign assistance funding -- the obligation and expenditure of large amounts of money in a short period of time -- it is referred to as the "action first" approach. The contrasting process approach emphasizes starting slowly and field-testing ideas prior to the introduction of large-scale interventions.

The blueprint approach, and the action-first variant,[8] assume that technology that is appropriate for a particular development undertaking can easily be transferred to another target population. They also assume the existence or easy creation of institutions capable of implementing a project. Further, they assume that information gaps can and must be filled prior to implmentation and that each and every activity to be carried out during the project can be specified, costed and scheduled in advance. There have been strong incentives for the use of conventional approaches in the design of AID's development projects.

The dichotomy between the "process" and "blueprint" approaches summarized above is admittedly extreme. In actual practice, projects are designed with some mix of these approaches in mind. However, for analytical purposes the distinction is useful because DAI's experience suggests that an approach which leans too far in the direction of the blueprint model often results in the manufacture of unfounded "estimated" data in order to accelerate project approval, and unrealistic implementation schedules and plans.

While there are legitimate differences of opinion over how much must be known before implementation can begin, and how quickly money can be effectively spent, recent research suggests that "development" is too complex a problem to be resolved with a few months of project design, followed by injection of funds.[9] Rather, the search for ways to bring lasting benefits to people at the bottom of the socioeconomic structure should persist over the entire life of the project. The thrust of the process approach is to structure the design and implementation of a project to encourage changes that will help an outside intervention (development assistance) to adapt to the local environment, culture and economy. This was the objective of DAI involvement in the design of twelve rural development projects.

This inquiry produced a better appreciation of how future projects aimed at small farmer populations might evolve: not in a haphazard or unpredictable fashion, but through modification and adaptation to their specific environments. By conventional criteria, the process approach would generate "unstructured" projects. But in a real sense, and because each project would have to operate in the context of budgets, schedules, personnel allotments, and so forth, there would be sufficient structure to guide those involved in preparing the initial project design, and subsequently in a continuing process of implementation, field-testing, and redesign.

The major components of the process approach, which optimally would be incorporated into a project design, are as follows:

- Designation of a preliminary period (sometimes referred to as a pre-implementation phase) to allow determination of detailed project activities;

- Explicit provision for flexibility during the implementation phase, in order to permit modification or redesign;
- Inclusion of mechanisms to promote small farmer participation in decisionmaking, specifically regarding project activities;
- Specific attention to ways of eliciting small farmer resource commitment to project activities;
- Focus on increasing the planning capacity and economic viability of local organizations; and
- Inclusion of an information system as an integral component, to assess project impact, identify problems, and indicate appropriate modifications in the design.

One finding of the *Strategies* report was the overriding importance of projects becoming self-sustaining, maintaining development benefits to the rural population after the withdrawal of foreign assistance. To do this, DAI recommended focusing primary attention on the establishment of income-generating activities.

Believing that the recommended "process" approach would make a useful contribution to AID in fulfilling the new Congressional directive, TAB extended the DAI contract to provide technical assistance to Missions in designing projects. In a letter to the AID Representative in Haiti, the Contract Monitor provided a good example of the conditions for such assistance:

> What we would expect from you and the Haitian Government in return is that you would agree to cooperate in developing the project along the lines which the research results indicate would be optimal for achieving local action involvement and project success. What we would like to do is to try to determine, with your help, whether applying what we know, or think we know, from our research makes a difference in terms of field project results. There will be no additional demand on USAID

staff; in fact, your burden should be lessened in that we will be making available highly qualified people to do a good bit of analysis and design work for you.[10]

Over the next two years DAI, under the TAB contract as well as other contractual arrangements, provided technical assistance in the design of twelve rural development projects.

To the staff of DAI this was as much a learning experience as it was a transfer of ideas to Missions in the field. While the *Strategies* report had generated a new basic orientation to project development, the assignments that followed provided first-hand experience in the design efforts required prior to implementing a "process" project. Insights were also gained into the strengths and weaknesses of the AID approval process, as well as the pitfalls of providing technical assistance to projects during implementation.

STRUCTURE OF THE REPORT

This study is divided into three parts. Section I, consisting of Chapters 1 through 5, relates the story of the twelve projects and the role DAI played in them. In this section, the empirical data drawn from the twelve projects are presented, the issues highlighted, and those conclusions drawn that seem reasonable given the limited sample. Reference documentation includes the official papers of the project, formal and informal memos and cable traffic, interviews with principal participants including AID personnel, other consultants and DAI's project design staff.[11] The analysis here is constrained by the examples in the project sample, but in Section II no such limitations are imposed, and the range of concern goes well beyond the data derived from the projects that were assisted in the past two years.

Chapter 1 gives a brief description of each project and sets out the circumstances of DAI involvement. Chapter 2 reports on the actual process of project design, paying particular attention to information requirements and the need for securing a working host country commitment to the key elements of each design. Chapter 3 leads the reader through the maze of the AID project review and approval process; it documents how two or more years can pass between project identification and project implementation, even when there are no substantive problems with the present design. Chapter 4 takes the reader through those projects that have reached the implementation stage; it discusses the problems that arise when implementation is inordinately delayed and when project designers and AID Missions brush lightly over critical details of project management and organization. Chapter 5 constitutes an attempt to define "success measures" for the twelve project designs and to conduct a qualitative and quantitative analysis of the determinants of success.

The review of the twelve project histories in Section I raises five broad issues of topical significance for project development and for the role of foreign assistance in delivering development benefits to the rural poor. These issues are discussed in the following four chapters. The twelve project designs that are chronicled in the first section are liberally referred to in Section II, but illustrations are also taken from other programs and projects that have been financed by AID.

Chapter 6 (the first in Section II) isolates and reflects on several procedural and substantive problems that are frequently encountered during the actual process of project design. These include information gathering, collaboration with host country government officials, composition of the design team, the availability and appropriateness of technology, and the need for adaptive field-testing. Chapter 7 analyzes the potential for and the limitations on "experimentation" in rural development projects, an issue that is a source of continuing controversy and delay in project review and approval. Chapter 8 examines the neglected issue of organizational arrangements for project implementation; it argues that projects more often fail for lack of attention to organizational rather than technical details, and makes a plea for a realignment of priorities so that AID Missions can worry more about how well project money is spent, rather than simply whether it is spent.

Chapter 9 examines the current AID project review and approval system, which frequently cannot distinguish good projects from bad, as well as the mechanisms currently employed that reduce the chances of successful project implementation. This chapter examines current initiatives to devolve greater authority to the field in order to rationalize and speed up project review and approval.

Section III consists of Conclusions and Recommendations.

NOTES

[1] For two of the best statements of this phenomenon and the reasons for it, see Keith Griffin, "Policy Options for Rural Development," background paper for the Ford Foundation Seminar on Rural Development and Employment, Ibadan, April 9-12, 1973, and Carl H. Gotsch, "Technical Change and the Distribution of Income in Rural Areas," *American Journal of Agricultural Economics,* 54:326-41, 1972. For more global treatments of the dynamics of the income phenomenon, see Montek S. Ahluwalia, "Income Inequality: Some Dimensions of the Problem," Chapter One in *Redistribution With Growth,* by Hollis Chenery et al., London: Oxford University Press, 1974; and Irma Adelman and Cynthia T. Morris, *Economic Growth and Social Equity in Developing Countries,* Stanford: Stanford University Press, 1973.

[2] Robert McNamara, President of the World Bank, "Address to the Board of Governors," Nairobi, Kenya, September 24, 1973.

[3] 1973 amendments to Chapter One, Section 102 of the Foreign Assistance Act of 1961.

[4] Various authors have criticized Congress for frequently being too general in its directives and thereby delegating too much policymaking authority to implementing bureaucracies, c.f., E. C. Hargrove, *The Missing Link*, Washington, D.C.: The Urban Institute, 1975; E. Bardach, *The Implementation Game*, Cambridge, Mass.: MIT Press, 1977; A. Wildavsky, *Politics of the Budgeting Process,* Boston: Little, Brown and Co., 1974; and M. Derthick, *New Towns in Town: Why a Program Failed*, Washington, D.C.: The Urban Institute, 1972.

[5] For a more detailed elaboration of this question, see Elliott R. Morss, "Testimony on Development Assistance Strategies for the Subcommittee on International Development of the House Committee on International Relations," November 28, 1977.

[6] Contract No. AID/CM/ta-C-73-41.

[7] E. R. Morss, J. K. Hatch, D. R. Mickelwait, C. F. Sweet, *Strategies for Small Farmer Development* (two volumes), Boulder, Colo.: Westview Press, 1976.

[8] These have been described in Development Alternatives, Inc., *Personnel Requirements for Project Development in East and Southern Africa,* prepared for REDSO/EA, October 17, 1977. This document will be referred to in subsequent citations as *Project Development in East and Southern Africa*.

[9] The *Strategies* report, among others, raised serious questions

about conventional approaches and formulated an alternative strategy capable of both identifying appropriate solutions and applying them. The empirical findings gathered during the *Strategies* study offered a number of valuable clues and insights. Generalizations were drawn for those cases in the sample where self-sustaining development did seem to be taking hold. The factors associated with this success were isolated and consideration was given to alternative methods of building those factors into future projects. This led to the specification of the process approach.

[10] Letter from the Technical Assistance Bureau, Office of Development Administration, dated August 14, 1975. The letter portrays DAI involvement as it might have been in Haiti, certainly not as it actually evolved.

[11] Since 1975 only one member of the senior professional staff has left DAI. The one design in which he participated included four other permanent DAI staff. All others involved in the twelve projects were available and interviewed for their insights, or became authors of various portions of this report.

I
Twelve Development Projects: Design, Approval, and Implementation

1 The Projects, Their Setting, and DAI Involvement

INTRODUCTION

During the period from September 1975 through July 1977, an even dozen projects in ten countries received project development assistance from DAI under various contractual arrangements with AID. Table 1.1 presents the formal project names, as taken from the last available official document, the country, identification numbers, and two ways of referring to the projects that will be used in the course of this report.

Of the twelve projects reviewed, eleven were approved by the formal review processes in Washington.[1] Three approved projects underwent major revisions in concept and approach after the DAI contributions were made, and one has been shelved until human rights issues are resolved.

In providing assistance to these projects, and then tracing their sometimes tortuous course through the review and approval process, a good deal has been learned about the problems and possibilities of designing and implementing development assistance projects that conform to the "New Directions" dictated by the 1975 Congressional mandate. The refocusing of the Agency appears to have been accepted by the vast majority of AID's professional staff. As might be expected, there has been considerable debate within the Agency over the current approach for bringing benefits to the rural poor. To highlight the issues in contention and to provide specifics of the contrasting strategies and proponents, case study material is drawn from the projects studied. The following summary presentations provide outline data on each of the twelve projects, including the current status as of January 1978.

TABLE 1.1

PROJECTS PROVIDED DESIGN ASSISTANCE, 1975-1977

Formal Name(s)	Country	Project No.	Cited As	Short Title
Rural Development Project Redesigned Phase I	Afghanistan	306-0131	Afghanistan Integrated Rural Development Project	Afghanistan
Small Farm Management and Technology	Chile	513-0313	Chile Farm Management Project	Chile
Small Farmer Development	Colombia	514-0203	Colombia Small Farmer Development Project	Colombia
Southern Gemu Gofa Area Rehabilitation	Ethiopia	663-0210	Ethiopia Rehabilitation Project	Ethiopia
District Planning/Rural Development (Phase I)	Ghana	641-0073	Ghana District Development Project	Ghana
Integrated Agricultural Development	Haiti	521-T-008	Haiti Integrated Agricultural Project	Haiti
Niamey Development Development - Phase I	Niger	683-0205	Niger Department Development Project	Niger
Agriculture Manpower Development	Tanzania	621-0119	Tanzania Farmer Training Project	Tanzania - FT
Arusha Planning/Village Development Project	Tanzania	621-0143	Tanzania Village Development Project	Tanzania - VD
Oncho Areas Village Development Fund	Upper Volta	686-0212	Upper Volta Oncho Project	Upper Volta - OP
Women's Roles in Development	Upper Volta	686-0211	Upper Volta Women's Project	Upper Volta - WP
North Shaba Maize Production	Zaire	660-0059	Zaire North Shaba Project	Zaire

AFGHANISTAN INTEGRATED RURAL DEVELOPMENT PROJECT

SUMMARY

Description [1]

The integrated rural development component of the Rural Works Project Amended (PP 2) will:

- Support the Rural Development Department's efforts to develop an area-specific rural development strategy; and
- Give the Mission access to the organizational setting of rural development in Afghanistan.

Total AID Funding

PP 2 $80,000 grant (IRD portion only) [2]

Duration

Five years

Design/Approval Process

	Document Submitted	DAI Involvement	Time Elapsed	Document Approved
PID	-	-	-	-
Rural Works PP	1/22/75	-	-	-
DAI Study	11/28/76	√	-	-
PP 1 [3]	1/29/77	-	-	-
PP 2	6/14/77	-	2 months	8/26/77
Pro/Ag Signed	-	-	1 month	9/18/77

Total Design/Approval Time

Rural Works PP through Project Agreement 2 years, 8 months

Status October 1977

The IRD portion of the project as designed is in limbo. Further action on the project will await the new Mission Director's review of the Afghanistan program and the posting of a new rural development officer to the country.

---

[1] The project description in the following case studies reflects the content of the last Project Paper.

[2] The funding level for the rural development component of PP 2 is estimated from the description of activities to be performed.

[3] Both PP 1, PP 2 are amendments to the Rural Works PP as defined herein.

CHILE FARM MANAGEMENT PROJECT

SUMMARY

Description

The project will improve the income of the newly titled land reform sector and other small farmers by providing subsidized farm management and new technology assistance through the private sector.

Total AID Funding

PP $2,600,000 loan

Duration

Two and one-half years

Design/Approval Process

	Document Submitted	DAI Involvement	Time Elapsed	Document Approved
IRR	2/75	-	-	-
Interim Report	5/3/76	✓	2 months	7/8/76
PP	5/31/77	✓	1 month	6/77

Total Design/Approval Time

IRR through PP   2 years, 4 months

Status October 1977

The project has been approved. However, The State Department has directed that all Agency assistance to Chile be suspended until the human rights issue can be resolved.

COLOMBIA SMALL FARMER DEVELOPMENT PROJECT

SUMMARY

<u>Description</u>

The project will develop replicable and eventually self-sustaining methods for increasing small farmer income and welfare, by devising ways to deliver critical services, including:

(a) improved agricultural technology,
(b) increased capabilities of small farmer organizations,
(c) development of appropriate technologies.

<u>Total AID Funding</u>

PP $3,400,000 loan

<u>Duration</u>

Three years

<u>Design/Approval Process</u>

	Document Submitted	DAI Involvement	Time Elapsed	Document Approved
IRR	1975	-	-	4/29/75
PP	12/5/75	✓	25 days	12/30/75
Loan Signed	-	-	6 months	6/14/76

<u>Total Design/Approval Time</u>

IRR through Loan 1 year, 2 months

<u>Status October 1977</u>

The implementing organization, ICA (Instituto Colombiano Agropecuario--the research and extension arm of the Colombian Ministry of Agriculture), initiated the project in January 1977.

ETHIOPIA REHABILITATION PROJECT

SUMMARY

Description

This is an experimental area development project aimed at improving the production and socioeconomic well-being of people living in drought-stricken areas. It will help develop capabilities of peasant associations and local government institutions to identify, plan and implement appropriate and cost-effective approaches to their environmental problems.

Total AID Funding

Mini-PP $197,000 grant PRP $3,169,886 grant

Duration

Eight months

Design/Approval Process

	Document Submitted	DAI Involvement	Time Elapsed	Document Approved
PID	6/6/76	-	-	6/76
PRP	12/6/76	√	4 months	4/77
Mini-PP	4/13/77	-	3 months	7/11/77

Total Design/Approval Time

PID to Mini-PP 1 year

Status October 1977

The pre-implementation phase of the project has begun with the assignment of a rural development specialist to provide planning assistance to the provincial administration.

GHANA DISTRICT DEVELOPMENT PROJECT

SUMMARY

Description

The project proposes to develop the ability of the Atebubu District Council, and its supporting system of local, regional and national institutions, to involve the population in planning, management, implementation and evaluation of a self-sustaining integrated rural development program.

Total AID Funding

PP Total	$7,180,000	Pre-Implementation Phase
Loan	$5,000,000	Grant $500,000
Grant	$2,180,000	

Duration

Four years (pre-implementation, one year; project activities, three years)

Design/Approval Process

	Document Submitted	DAI Involvement	Time Elapsed	Document Approved
PID	7/3/75	-	2 months	9/27/75
PRP 1	5/28/76	✓	-	-
PRP 2	9/3/76	✓	1 month	Rejected 10/15/76
PP	4/21/77	-	2 months	6/27/77
Grant Signed [1]	-	-	-	7/77

Total Design/Approval Time

PID to Grant Signature — 2 years

Status October 1977

The Mission submitted a scope of work for competitive bidding on the pre-implementation phase of the project last July. This was advertised in the *Commerce Business Daily* on October 25, 1977.

[1] Funding for the entire project has been authorized, but the grant agreement only obligates funds for the pre-implementation phase of the project. The rest of the project will be incrementally funded.

HAITI INTEGRATED AGRICULTURAL PROJECT

SUMMARY

Description

The project will develop the institutional capacity of the Ministry of Agriculture, Natural Resources and Rural Development (DARNDR), as well as of community organizations, to deliver the following production resources and services to small farmers: agricultural extension/information, irrigation, soil conservation, research and development, agricultural credit and training.

Total AID Funding

PPs (first and second)
Grant $4,100,000
Loan $8,000,000

Duration

Five years

Design/Approval Process

	Document Submitted	DAI Involvement	Time Elapsed	Document Approved
PID	8/75	-	-	-
DAI Paper	12/75	✓	-	-
PP 1	7/29/76	✓	-	-
PP 2	9/22/76	-	5 days	9/27/76
Loan Signed	-	-	7 months	4/27/77

Total Design/Approval Time

PID to Loan Signature 1 year, 8 months

Status October 1977

After the loan agreement was signed, the Mission requested that the loan portion be switched to a grant, which was authorized. At the end of August no funds had been disbursed. The loan portion of the project was switched to a grant as have been all funds in Haiti. Compliance with the Conditions Precedent of the grant agreement has been extended to December 1977, and no funds can be disbursed until they have been met.

NIGER DEPARTMENT DEVELOPMENT PROJECT

SUMMARY

Description[1]

The project will begin a process of rural development in the Department of Niamey by strengthening agricultural services, training farmers, developing cooperatives, livestock, irrigation, information programs, and preparing a comprehensive area development program.

Total AID Funding

Mission PP $4,699,000 grant

Duration

Three years

Design/Approval Process

	Document Submitted	DAI Involvement	Time Elapsed	Document Approved
PID	-	-	-	6/75
PRP	12/75	-	1 month	1/8/76
PP 1	8/76	✓		
PP 2	3/4/77	-	2 months	5/25/77
Pro/Ag Signed	-	-	3 months	8/29/77

Total Design/Approval Time

PID to Project Agreement 2 years, 2 months

Status October 1977

A project manager was hired in May 1977, before the project agreement was signed. He was paid out of Mission funds and instructed to begin preparation for project activities. The project agreement was signed in August 1977.

---

[1] For purposes of consistency, AID posts in the Sahelian countries are referred to as Missions and the representatives as Mission Directors, although these terms are not technically correct.

TANZANIA FARMER TRAINING PROJECT

SUMMARY

Description

The project will improve the social and economic well-being of small farmers by gaining an understanding of their decisionmaking practices and constraints and by testing different technological packages, and training and extension approaches.

Total AID Funding

PP $2,514,150 grant

Duration

Four years

Design/Approval Process

	Document Submitted	DAI Involvement	Time Elapsed	Document Approved
PID	-	-	-	-
PRP 1	1/75	-	-	-
PRP 2	10/24/75	✓	2 months	12/10/75
PP	3/29/76	✓	16 months	8/8/77
Pro/Ag Signed			1 month	9/13/77

Total Design/Approval Time

PRP to Project Agreement   2 years, 8 months

Status October 1977

The request for competitive bidding to implement this project will be published in *The Commerce Business Daily* shortly.

TANZANIA VILLAGE DEVELOPMENT PROJECT

SUMMARY

Description

The project will help the villages in Arumeru, Mbulu and Hanang Districts of the Arusha Region to identify, implement and evaluate development activities for improving production, income and well-being of small farmers.

Total AID Funding

PP $14,660,000 grant

Duration

Four years

Design/Approval Process

	Document Submitted	DAI Involvement	Time Elapsed	Document Approved
PID	11/30/76	-	3 months	3/9/77
PP 1	7/77	✓	-	-
PP 2	4/15/78	✓	12 months	7/7/78

Total Design/Approval Time

PID to PP Approval 19 months

Status June 1978

The first PP was approved on the condition that the Village Development Project and Arusha Regional planning exercises be integrated, that additional data be collected for the road and water activities to satisfy 611(a) requirements, that criteria be established upon which to assess other subprojects, and that separate initial environmental evaluations be done on each subproject. The second PP contained detailed costing estimates required to satisfy 611(a).

UPPER VOLTA ONCHO PROJECT

SUMMARY

Description

The project will build the organizational and financial capabilities of villages recently settled in areas freed of onchocerciasis, through the identification and development of local, income-generating enterprises.

Total AID Funding

PP $2,173,000 grant

Duration

Four years

Design/Approval Process

	Document Submitted	DAI Involvement	Time Elapsed	Document Approved
PID	1975	-	-	10/17/75
PRP	11/20/75	√	1 month	12/17/75
PP	6/28/76	√	15 months	9/7/77

Total Design/Approval Time

PID to PP Approval 2 years

Status October 1977

The PP was approved; final authorization awaits Congressional approval of the new Foreign Assistance Appropriation.

UPPER VOLTA WOMEN'S PROJECT

SUMMARY

Description

The project is designed to improve the quality of life in Upper Volta villages by developing the capabilities of rural women to plan and implement economic production activities.

Total AID Funding

PP $1,056,000 grant

Duration

Three years

Design/Approval Process

	Document Submitted	DAI Involvement	Time Elapsed	Document Approved
PID	5/75	-	1 month	6/75
PRP	12/12/75	-	2 months	2/19/76
PP 1	6/28/76	-	-	Rejected
PP 2	1/77	✓	2 months	3/11/77
Grant Ag Signed				9/30/77

Total Design/Approval Time

PID to Grant Agreement   2 years, 4 months

Status October 1977

When the project was approved, the Mission hired an advisor to begin background preparation for the project implementation. Now that the grant has been signed, full implementation should begin shortly.

ZAIRE NORTH SHABA PROJECT

SUMMARY

Description

The project is designed to develop a replicable process for improving small farmer production and income by testing and introducing improved maize and other crop technologies, by developing farmer organizations, by identifying and producing improved agricultural implements and processing equipment, by expanding market services, by rehabilitating rural roads, and by developing the planning, management and evaluation capabilities of government agencies.

Total AID Funding

PP
Loan $3,340,000
Grant $5,964,000

Duration

Two years, eight months

Design/Approval Process

	Document Submitted	DAI Involvement	Time Elapsed	Document Approved
PID	12/12/74	-	-	-
PRP	3/76	-	2 months	5/10/76
PP	9/17/76	✓	13 days	9/30/76
Pro/Ag Signed				9/30/76

Total Design/Approval Time

PID to Project Agreement 1 year, 10 months

Status October 1977

The implementing team is in Zaire, working on the first stage of the project.

THE PROJECT DESIGN ENVIRONMENT

The circumstances under which DAI began work on project design differed a great deal from project to project. The circumstances included differences in host country and Mission commitment to the "New Directions" mandate and the degree of decisionmaking with respect to the elements of the project that had already been completed.

Host Country and AID Commitment to New Directions Development

The developing world varies greatly in approaches to the problems and priorities of development assistance. This becomes particularly apparent when the beneficiaries of the assistance are to be, by AID directive, among the least educated, powerful or affluent. In some countries, AID can offer support to national plans that have already been formulated. In others, there have been serious problems in the identification of overlapping goals (host country's and AID's), and some countries have been willing to accept small farmer or rural development project assistance for reasons other than national dedication to assisting the poorest of the poor.

Table 1.2 presents DAI's judgments, in the ten countries where projects were designed, of each government's general commitment to a redistribution of income as a goal of development assistance.[2] These judgments may be challenged and positions along the continuum revised, but few can argue that there are not vast differences in host government priorities and plans when going from Tanzania or Ethiopia to Haiti. Such differences may affect host country agreement on the design, the collaborative effort, and the commitment to implement the project as designed. The lack of a strong host country commitment to assisting the poorest of the poor did not prevent the *design* of a project consistent with the "New Directions." It simply aggravated an already difficult task.[3]

The attitudes of the USAID Missions toward the implementation of bottom-up development targeted at the rural poor were positive, with one exception.[4] Only in Tanzania in 1975, during the design of the Farmer Training Project, was there evidence of a failure to support the New Directions philosophy. This was due in part to the position of the Ambassador, who wished to restrict the size of the USAID staff, as well as to the influence of a contract team, which

TABLE 1.2

HOST COUNTRY COMMITMENT TO AID'S NEW DIRECTIONS

Country	Strong Commitment	Limited Commitment	Expedient Commitment
Afghanistan		X	
Chile		X	
Colombia		X	
Ethiopia	X		
Ghana		X	
Haiti			X
Niger		X	
Tanzania	X		
Upper Volta		X	
Zaire			X

Judgments based upon:

- Relative proportion of national government funds invested in the agriculture sector.
- Price, tax, and/or import policies that discriminate against or support the agriculture sector.
- Relative support to small farm sector within agricultural programs.
- Observations and discussions with working-level government officials during design team visits.

played a major role in coordination between the Ministry of Agriculture and USAID, and had not been persuaded of the need for redirection of more traditional efforts at institutional and infrastructure support. By the time of the second design effort in Tanzania, nearly two years later, the USAID Mission was solidly behind local area targeting and decentralization, which form the basis for most rural development assistance.

Preexisting Conditions in Project Identification and Design

In all cases, the process approach was introduced to the design process after project identification (the PID) and other decisionmaking had already taken place. Obviously serious difficulties arise in the completion of a process approach design in the face of prior decisions by both the host country and AID. In those instances where the process model was not well-understood and/or appreciated, a great deal of time was spent in discussions with AID staff and host country officials. The "collaboration" requirement was high, and a lack of sufficient time to discuss the concept and convince AID staff and host country officials of the utility of this approach was evidenced in the implementation stage, when this was reached.

Five of the projects had predetermined the implementing agency and the project management arrangements (Table 1.3, Column 1). Of these five, two were subsequently modified (Afghanistan and Chile) during the course of project design. There were minor changes in project areas (Column 2) in Tanzania - FT, Tanzania - VD and Zaire, adjusting as the project moved from identification to a more detailed planning phase, with six project areas unchanged during design. The specification of project components (Column 3), which is shorthand for prior determination of the direction or thrust of the project, was a significant problem in those projects where a conventional design approach had already been accepted. Of the seven projects that had undergone prior decisionmaking, three (Chile, Colombia and Ghana) required no fundamental changes in direction or project thrust. However, in the remaining four (Haiti, Niger, Tanzania - FT and Zaire), significant changes were recommended by the DAI-assisted design teams.

Project Review Papers (PRPs) had been completed for three of the four projects before DAI's arrival (Column 5). In Zaire the process approach was

TABLE 1.3

PREEXISTING CONDITIONS
AT THE TIME OF DAI'S ENTRY INTO THE PROJECT

Project	(1) Implementing Agency Specified	(2) Project Area Specified	(3) Project Components Specified	(4) Project Dollar Target Specified	(5) PRP Completed
Afghanistan	Yes	No	No	No	No
Chile	Yes	Yes	Yes	Yes	No
Colombia	Yes	No	Yes	Yes	No
Ethiopia	No	Yes	No	No	No
Ghana	No	Yes	Yes	No	No
Haiti	No	Yes	Yes	No	No
Niger	No	Yes	Yes	Yes	Yes
Tanzania - FT	Yes	Yes	Yes	Yes	Yes
Tanzania - VD	No	Yes	No	Yes	No
Upper Volta - OP	Yes	Yes	No	No	No
Upper Volta - WP	No	No	No	Yes	Yes
Zaire	No	Yes	Yes	Yes	Yes

Columns: (1) Positive responses mean not only that the overall ministry was identified at the national level, but that project management had been determined.

(2) All projects had an area focus, although in some cases it was not identified prior to the arrival of the design team.

(3) Identification of the overriding problem to be solved and a determination or broad outline of the solution had been made.

(4) All projects had nominal dollar limits imposed by prior paperwork. Here the question is whether DAI operated under a requirement that the project be at a certain dollar obligation level.

accepted, and the changes in the project resulted in major modifications of activities to be carried out, based upon a closer examination of the environment in North Shaba. In Tanzania, the Farmer Training Project became embroiled in a disagreement over appropriate technical assistance for a rural development program, holding up project approval for nearly sixteen months. In both Haiti and Niger the approach used by DAI was not accepted by the Missions, and implementation reverted to a conventional blueprint or action-first model.

Review of the twelve projects suggests that the chance of successfully employing a process approach for project design depends significantly upon the development philosophy of the host country and implementing agencies, early involvement of the designers in project development -- well before the PRP or PP is formulated -- and a Mission Director who is, if not sympathetic, at least willing to be convinced of the utility of the new design concepts.

DAI INVOLVEMENT IN THE DESIGN PROCESS

The twelve projects studied represent a wide spectrum of DAI involvement in the project design process. This includes not only the resources committed in relation to other actors in the project design process, but the mandate given to DAI by the AID Missions. Since this was a learning process for DAI, as well as a test of the implementability of the process approach to project development, the chronology of project involvement is important in examining the completed project designs.

DAI Resources Used in the Design Process

DAI provided fifty percent of the total non-Mission resources used in designing the twelve projects.[5] The average involvement per project was thirteen person-weeks and two trips. This was inflated by the very large design effort in Chile, involving seven trips and nearly forty-three person-weeks of DAI design time. Three senior designers were responsible for the leadership in all twelve projects. Table 1.4 provides the details of these calculations.

TABLE 1.4

RESOURCE COMMITMENTS FOR PROJECT DESIGN

	Person-Weeks								
	DAI[1]	Other Non-AID	AID/W and REDSO	Mission[2]	Total U.S.	Design Leadership	No. DAI Design Trips	No. DAI Team Members	Special Circumstances
Afghanistan	22.6	0	0.6	6	29.2	DAI Designated	1	4	Local-hire team assisted in community, household and women's surveys during field data collection exercise, a total of 51 person-weeks.
Chile	42	0	9	3	54	Early work DAI emerged PRP/PP DAI Designated	7	5	A special consultant team was hired for the host country agency, a pilot test was conducted of the project's concepts, and numerous special studies completed.
Colombia	2.5	6.5	1	12	22.1	Mission/DAI emerged	2	2	There was strong Mission involvement in all aspects of the project; DAI contributed a design for the project components and the monitoring and evaluating section.
Ethiopia	11.2	6	8	5	30.2	DAI Designated	1	2	DAI was given veto over non-Mission design team members. Ongoing design efforts funded under implementation phase are not included.
Ghana	10.1	-	-	9	19.1	DAI Designated	3	3	
Haiti	8.4	28	14	12	62.4	PP AID/W	2	4	DAI completed a special study prior to PP design. During PP design DAI's process approach did not carry the day.
Niger	5.4	16	1	4	26.4	DAI Designated	1	1	DAI worked on first PP only. Subsequent revisions did not involve DAI.
Tanzania - FT	5.2	-	5	2	12.2	DAI emerged	2	2	DAI worked from a rejected PRP. The second PRP involved DAI, as did the PP, which was written in Washington.
Tanzania - VD	11.4	26	-	4	41.4	DAI Designated	1	3	Local-hire anthropologists/sociologists undertook field data collection based on DAI information requirements outline.
Upper Volta - OP	10.8	5	4	5	24.8	PRP DAI emerged PP DAI Designated	2	3	
Upper Volta - WP	15.6	-	2	4	21.6	DAI Designated	1	5	
Zaire	11.3	19	15.9	8	54.2	PP AID/W and DAI	1	2	Two local U.S. anthropologists in project area assisted in field data collection.
TOTAL	156.6	106.5	60.5	74	397.6				
AVERAGE	13.05	8.88	5.04	6.17	33.13				

[1] DAI time from travel records; other time estimated.

[2] Mission time includes only that directly associated with the design team. No attempt was made to capture the in-house review or other normal project development requirements.

The Activities and Responsibilities of the Design Team

The original mandate given by the Mission and the responsibilities that evolved over the course of project design were markedly different among the twelve projects. In some, DAI was asked to develop a reiterative design in collaboration with host country officials, to ensure that the data for justification of the project to AID/Washington and the host country planners were obtained and packaged as necessary, and to help conduct the negotiations with and obtain the commitment from the appropriate host country policymakers and decisionmakers. In other projects, DAI undertook only a portion of the overall responsibilities.

Table 1.5 presents, by project, the activities undertaken by DAI during the design process.

In six of the twelve designs, DAI undertook all activities, including a major part in the negotiations with the host government's policymakers. Any design flaws in these projects, lack of collaboration, lack of supporting data, or an inconclusive commitment by the host country would ultimately rest on the DAI designers, barring any intervening factors that were critical in the design process. All factors -- those already discussed, the actual design process and outcome, and the review and approval process -- are taken together and analyzed for important determinants in Chapter 5.

The Costs of Project Design

In 1977 dollars (after October 1, 1977, federal pay readjustments), thirteen person-weeks of DAI design time averaged slightly under $20,000. Taking the average per diem rates paid in the ten countries, and the weighted average of roundtrip costs, DAI involvement cost approximately $28,000 per project. Costing the "AID non-Mission" contribution at the same rates, reducing the "other non-AID" components to seventy-five percent of the DAI costs, and eliminating the travel and per diem for the Mission contribution, the average design utilized thirty-three person-weeks and cost more than $62,000.[6] This is not the total cost, of course, since some of the projects had previous design teams, and several had follow-on redesign efforts, which are not included in the calculations.[7]

TABLE 1.5

DAI ACTIVITIES DURING THE DESIGN PHASE

Project	Design	Working-Level Collaboration	Data for Justification	Packaging for Approval	Negotiation With Host Country Decisionmakers
Afghanistan	X	X	X	-	+
Chile	X	X	+	+	-
Colombia	X	+	-	-	-
Ethiopia	X	X	X	X	+
Ghana	X	X	-	X	-
Haiti PP[1]	+	-	-	+	-
Niger	X	X	X	X	+
Tanzania - FT	X	X	+	+	+
Tanzania - VD	X	X	X	X	+
Upper Volta - OP	X	X	X	X	+
Upper Volta - WP	X	X	X	X	+
Zaire	X	X	X	X	+

Code: X = Primary involvement under the overall direction of the Mission.

+ = Shared involvement under the overall direction of the Mission.

- = Little or no involvement.

---

[1] DAI contributions used in project design were limited to the exposition of the monitoring and evaluation system for the project.

Source of Funds for Project Design

DAI's contribution to the design of the twelve projects came from a mixture of AID/Washington and Mission funding. Although it could be surmised that "free technical assistance" might be discounted by the Missions, it would appear that the funding source was not important in terms of the firm's influence on the design process.

TABLE 1.6

FUNDING SOURCE FOR DAI'S DESIGN ASSISTANCE

Project	AID/Washington	Mission
Afghanistan		X
Chile	X	
Colombia	X	
Ethiopia		X
Ghana	X	
Haiti	X	
Niger		X
Tanzania - FT	X	
Tanzania - VD		X
Upper Volta - OP		X
Upper Volta - WP		X
Zaire		X

The Chronology of DAI Design Involvement

DAI's learning process began with the field research that led to the publication of the *Strategies* report. Over the course of the next several years, the principal designers gained increasing sophistication in the components of bottom-up rural development projects and in the collaboration necessary to ensure that the projects have some positive chance of being implemented by the host country as designed.

Table 1.7 presents the chronology of DAI involvement by project and principal designers.

TABLE 1.7

CHRONOLOGY OF DAI INVOLVEMENT
BY PROJECT AND PRINCIPAL DESIGNER

Project	Date of Initial Involvement	Principal Designer
Tanzania - FT	September 1975	Sweet
Chile	October 1975	Mickelwait
Haiti	October 1975	Sweet/Morss
Upper Volta - OP	October 1975	Sweet
Colombia	November 1975	Mickelwait
Ghana	November 1975	Sweet
Upper Volta - WP	March 1976	Sweet
Niger	May 1976	Sweet
Zaire	July 1976	Sweet/Roth
Afghanistan	October 1976	Mickelwait/Roth
Ethiopia	October 1976	Sweet
Tanzania - VD	May 1977	Sweet/Weisel

NOTES

[1] This report is current through January 1978. Some late information up to June 1978 has been included.

[2] While few countries engage in major income redistribution from a fixed national income, many are willing to allow the percentage shares of growth in income to accrue to the poor. This division of a growing pie is generally thought to be more politically palatable than major shifts in the control of wealth or productive assets, as represented by an effective land reform program.

[3] The question of implementing projects in countries that only weakly support the "New Directions" is discussed in Chapter 8.

[4] This is not to say that all Missions agreed with the DAI approach, a subject that is discussed in following pages. Nor did all Mission staff believe in the approach. Policymakers quickly fell in line and couched their funding requests in language of "benefit incidence." Lack of cooperation was more often found at the technical-staff level.

[5] This resource count includes only those activities in which DAI was involved.

[6] Calculated on an average salary of $29,156, with a fully loaded average daily rate of $248, six days per week. Per diem

averaged $46 per day and the weighted average of travel costs is $1,164 per trip, four trips per project.

[7] The costs of designing these twelve projects were significantly lower than those for non-process designs in East and Southern Africa. There the average for four projects that were intended to deliver services to a rural target population was 104.9 person-weeks, as three of the projects involved large study teams. *Project Development in East and Southern Africa,* op. cit., Annex J, P. J-4, Table J-3, subtracting three DAI process design projects -- Tanzania - FT, Tanzania - VD, and Southern Gamu Gofa.

2
The Process of Project Design

INTRODUCTION

In ten of the twelve projects, the creation of a design was an evolutionary process, which began with the identification of the development problem or task. Often this consisted of the designation of a local area to be developed or a local population to be assisted. A next step was the specification of critical design issues to be resolved and a determination of what information would be necessary to resolve them. This was followed by drawing up data points to be filled and deciding upon a strategy for collecting and analyzing the data.

This chapter begins with an examination of the time spent by the design teams in discrete activities during project design. Then two key activities, information collection and collaboration with host country officials, are discussed in greater detail.

TIME SPENT ON PROJECT DESIGN ACTIVITIES

According to DAI's estimates, shown in Table 2.1, the twelve design teams spent on average roughly 43 percent of their time preparing project documentation. This left about 24 percent of total time for discussing and negotiating ideas with host country government officials. Project development time was particularly high in two cases. In Afghanistan this was due to the formal survey work conducted by the team; in Haiti it was because AID gathered together some twenty specialists to assemble a project. Neither approach proved very useful for project design.[1]

TABLE 2.1

USE OF DESIGN TIME [1]

Project	Total Design Team Time (Person-Weeks)	Percent of Total Design Team Time Spent in: (1) Project Development	(2) Project Packaging	(3) Collabo-ration	(4) Negotia-tion
Afghanistan	29.2	80	10	8	2
Chile	54	40	15	40	5
Colombia	22.1	50	40	5	5
Ethiopia	30.2	40	25	30	5
Ghana	19.1	40	50	5	5
Haiti	62.4	50	40	5	5
Niger	26.4	20	45	30	5
Tanzania - FT	12.2	40	15	40	5
Tanzania - VD	41.4	35	30	30	5
Upper Volta - OP	24.8	35	40	23	2
Upper Volta - WP	21.6	40	40	15	5
Zaire	54.2	45	45	8	2

Column: (1) Project development is the amount of time spent generating and analyzing information for project design.

(2) Project packaging is the amount of time spent preparing the project justifications and writing the documentation.

(3) Project collaboration is the amount of time spent discussing and shaping the project design with host country officials.

(4) Project negotiation is the amount of time spent in getting the formal agreement of key decisionmakers for the project.

[1] For a discussion of the relationship between quality of a project design and the time spent on various activities of the review/approval process see Chapter Five.

INFORMATION FOR PROJECT DESIGN

The amount and type of information collected and analyzed for the design of the twelve projects differed according to the existing information base and the design team's mandate and resources. There was almost no field data collection in some designs; in others comprehensive data bases were developed through formal surveys; in still other projects, information was collected through rapid survey techniques.[2] The following section describes the experience with information collection and analysis that took place in the twelve design exercises.

Experience with Project Design Information Collection and Analysis

Figure 2.1 shows, for each project, the existing information base and the information generated during project design. Table 2.2 presents information on the amount of time taken to satisfy information requirements during project design. This is presented in terms of "levels of intensity" ratings, where 1 signifies low intensity (i.e., very little time was spent in information gathering) and 5 signifies high intensity (i.e., a relatively large amount of time was spent in information gathering). This is further broken out by source of data.

Five projects were rated low on initial field reconnaissance, but the circumstances varied considerably. In Ghana there was little field investigation, in line with the project implementation timetable -- a district development project prepared in two phases to allow the unknowns to be identified and resolved prior to the second phase. In Afghanistan the data collection effort focused on structured surveys rather than field reconnaissance, although the village-leaders interviews reflected many of the aspects and content of the rapid survey technique used in Africa. In Chile, with its well-developed local institutions, the preferred data collection technique was a pilot test of the major concepts of the development project. This resolved many of the details of implementation that had remained unresolved at the conclusion of the initial investigation.[3] In Haiti DAI conducted a ten-day field trip into the project area. This was the extent of the firm's involvement in data collection, as the project was subsequently designed using a different development approach. In Niger there was limited field reconnaissance, which was a definite handicap to the appropriate design of local institutions.

FIGURE 2.1

EXISTING INFORMATION BASE AND INFORMATION GENERATED BY DAI, BY PROJECT

Project	Existing Information Base	Information Generated During Project Design[1]
Colombia	Agricultural sector survey, series of social and economic studies.	Since local areas had not been identified, information was only collected to apply model in Colombian context.
Haiti	Almost none on target population and local environment. Many engineering studies.	Preliminary reconnaissance of area to identify development potentials and possible alternatives.[2]
Ghana	Profile data on selected district, compiled by local and AID officials.	Analysis of the new local government setup and government development priorities.
Chile	General agricultural, social and economic studies; small farmer production survey; special studies of the land reform sector farmer.	Pilot test case was established to resolve such "unknowns" as the appropriate institutional structure and the need for credit.
Tanzania - FT	Almost none.	Detailed information on institutional capabilities of agricultural training institutes and how course content related to small farmer needs.
Niger	Secondary source material with statistics on project area.	Preliminary field reconnaissance, detailed area profile information, social/economic/technical information justification.
Upper Volta-OP	UN, IBRD, FAO background studies of resettlement program, farm records for all resettled villages.	Field survey of representative resettlement villages. Village meetings on possible project activities. Data on existing village-level enterprises.

[1] In Haiti and Niger the design process continued after DAI completed substantive inputs.

[2] One ten-day trip, including a week in the field early in project formation, was the limit of DAI involvement until the actual writing of the PP.

FIGURE 2.1 (Continued)

Project	Existing Information Base	Information Generated During Project Design
Upper Volta - WP	FAO and local social science research reports on Women in Development.	Formal survey of villages in four regions to determine decision-making and participation roles of women. Preliminary cost/benefit analyses of micro-development projects. Village meetings.
Ethiopia	Area-specific studies done by local anthropologists, identifying development potentials. AID documentation of relief activities.	Intensive survey of project area, identifying production potentials, the support system, the local economic and social infrastructure. Data on provincial and national programs. Village meetings.
Tanzania - VD	Area-specific studies done by social scientists using DAI data collection guide.	Intensive survey of project area, identifying production potentials and constraints, social and economic infrastructure requirements. Intensive farmer interviews on practices and constraints. Subsequent data collection on costs of road and water system construction.
Zaire	Documentation on project area provided by Department of Agriculture and by nine-member AID design team.	Intensive survey of project area covering social, economic, political and infrastructure systems. Farmer interviews and group meetings in 120 villages. Macro-economic and pricing data.
Afghanistan	Almost none.[1]	Village survey, household survey with comprehensive data collection instrument. Survey on women in rural development.

[1] In the Afghanistan case, the existing information base included a demographic survey, aerial photographs, an agricultural census and an anthropological study. Unfortunately, the information was of little use in designing a project for the specific district that had been selected for a pilot test. The demographic survey, after extrapolation, did allow a rough estimate of the total population of the area. To be consistent with the other projects, only information that was directly used in the project design has been indicated.

TABLE 2.2

LEVEL OF INTENSITY OF DATA COLLECTION IN PROJECT DESIGN

Project	Field Reconnaissance	Secondary Sources	Project-Specific Surveys/Farm Records
Afghanistan	2	0	5
Chile	2	4	5
Colombia	None	4	None
Ethiopia	5	4	None
Ghana	1	1	None
Haiti	2	0	None
Niger	2	2	None
Tanzania - FT	3	0	None
Tanzania - VD	5	0	None
Upper Volta - OP	3	2	5
Upper Volta - WP	3	1	3
Zaire	5	0	None

Code: 1 = Low intensity; 5 = high intensity.
0 = Little of specific value for the project although general documentation was reviewed.

In the other design exercises, more intensive field data collection and analysis took place. Different techniques were employed, producing information that ranged from essential to non-useful for project design. Local-hire social scientists were asked to prepare in-depth studies of specific areas for the preparation of two projects: the Ethiopia Rehabilitation Project and the Tanzania Village Development Project. In the Ethiopia project, three out of the four papers were written with no guidance on the types of information needed for the design of area development projects; this resulted in important gaps in the information base, especially on the ways in which production decisions were made at family and village levels. The point here is not whether "information" per se is useful; rather that information to be useful must be responsive to design needs. In the Ethiopia case, the utility of the information contained in these papers was significantly reduced because they were written without inputs or guidance from the designers.

The background papers for both Tanzania projects were prepared with critical questions and data requirements specified. Both sets of background papers yielded excellent descriptions that helped identify project ideas. Considerable interaction with the local population and officials was still needed to actually shape the resulting designs, but this interaction was facilitated greatly when the social scientists who had done the background work were also involved in the actual design effort.

While these background papers were thus exceedingly useful, in the case of the Tanzania - VD project additional data to meet 611(a) requirements were requested by the Project Committee. This resulted in trips to Tanzania by both AID and REDSO engineers to gather technical data on road and water development a number of months after the initial PP was submitted for approval.

In the Afghanistan Integrated Rural Development Project, the design team attempted three major, census-type surveys. The first was a village survey where key village leaders were involved in group interviews; the second was a household survey; and the third was a survey of women, designed and carried out in large part by Muslim professional women. These efforts generated a massive data base, but the time allocated for project design permitted only a superficial analysis. A considerable amount of "static" information was generated, which proved helpful for packaging and presentation purposes, but almost useless in the process of project design.[4]

The structured survey developed for the Upper Volta Women's Project was far more limited in scope than those tried in Afghanistan. This instrument attempted to gather information on the decisionmaking and participation roles of women in villages in four parts of the country. It generated a body of data that was used for project justification in the social, economic and technical analyses. It also ensured that the project design team members focused on the same set of concerns, since the team split up to cover different parts of the country. However, the information needed for the design of the project components was generated through a series of informal discussions with groups of village women, as well as with local-level extension workers and government officials.

Rapid survey techniques were used in the field investigations for the Upper Volta Oncho Project, the Tanzania Village Development Project, the Ethiopia Rehabilitation Project and the Zaire North Shaba Project. The rapid survey technique differs from census surveys in that questions are asked only until there is certainty in answers from each source, including individual farmers, village groups, local leaders, merchants and government officials.[5] As the knowledge base expands, the questions are changed to solicit further information and ideas for project development. During this process the information is synthesized in the minds of the design team, which makes the data collection and analysis virtually nonduplicative. The emphasis is on the collection of the information necessary to understand the dynamics of a local situation. This helps in formulating hypotheses about the probable impact of various interventions with an increased capacity to specify necessary resources over a longer period of time (about three years).

The investigation for the Upper Volta Oncho Project revealed a major weakness in the resettlement program: a lack of mechanisms for building village organizational and financial capabilities. This was especially critical, since the government had decided to introduce families from different ethnic groups into the same village. Data collection then focused on the identification of possible ways to strengthen local-level leadership. In contrast, the requirements for developing the areas covered by the Zaire and Tanzania projects extended from applied technological research, to the strengthening of several aspects of the agricultural support system, to the rehabilitation or construction of major economic infrastructure. The field investigations were therefore intensive, so that a reasonable estimate of needed resources could be made.

In Zaire, Ethiopia, and Upper Volta, a primary collection technique was informal meetings with village groups. These discussions proved to be a valuable resource for generating project ideas and, as they emerged, for getting feedback or farmer reactions to the ideas. As has been mentioned earlier, attempts to initiate this type of dialogue were ineffective in Afghanistan, because the information flow, for sociocultural and methodological reasons, was not reciprocal.

Conclusions Concerning Information Collection for Project Design

Based on experience with the twelve projects, certain preliminary conclusions can be drawn regarding information collection and analysis in the design process.

First a lack of intensive field data collection during the design phase need not result in unsound projects. If Missions were allotted funds to spend for New Directions projects, the collection of data for project design could end when sufficient information is collected to ensure that implementation can begin with:

- A specification of the goals and objectives of the project;
- A determination of an area and target group;
- A preliminary decision on implementation arrangements; and
- A budget for operations during the initial stages.

Information collection should continue throughout the implementation phase of a project in any case. Under the present AID project design system, considerable data are collected during the design phase, primarily to satisfy the criteria for project approval rather than for use in substantive design formulation.[6] Intensive field data collection allows a specification of longer-term resource requirements for project development, but is not essential for the initiation of projects that have this process built into a pre-implementation phase.

Clearly the more relevant information that is available, the better; but data collection and analysis have significant attendant costs too, which means that marginal costs and benefits have to be considered. In this regard, a very general guideline can be laid down: the more ambitious and complex the project activities are, the more information is needed as a prerequisite. Although it is possible to start with almost any level of information when relying on the process approach, the initial complexity of project activities should be governed by the quality and quantity of baseline information.

The experience with specific techniques of data collection yielded mixed results: In general:

- If the design team's initial information requirements are specified, background papers prepared can speed the process of project design, providing a strong foundation for identifying possible interventions.
- Undirected or academically oriented research and census-type surveys produce data that are useful for project justification, but do not necessarily contribute to the actual project design.
- Rapid-survey techniques, which involve village groups and other sources of information in a dialogue, illuminate the dynamics of interactions and help to define options for project content.
- Pilot projects can be very useful in testing unresolved deficiencies in the design process, but require nearly as much attention as a pre-implementation phase which is a preferred start-up activity.

COLLABORATION IN PROJECT DESIGN

Gaining A Host Country Commitment

The commitment of host country agencies to a project is as critical as the actual shaping of the project design. Early on in each DAI design assignment it was necessary to reach agreement with key national agencies regarding the project goals and the development approach to be employed. Within this conceptual framework, the next step (if fieldwork was involved) was to share in the shaping of project ideas through the collaborative involvement (normally through group meetings) of both local officials and potential beneficiaries in the areas of project concentration.[7] Project ideas were developed and refined, starting at the bottom of the structure, up through each administrative level, to the key national decisionmakers.

In most of the twelve projects, collaboration took place both in the project areas and at the national level. Through discussions of current practices and major problems or constraints with knowledgeable local sources, it was possible to identify elements that had to be built into a project. Particularly useful were the reactions of farmer groups and other local sources to the alternatives formulated by the design team.

The best illustrations of this process are provided by the two Tanzania projects and the Ethiopia Rehabilitation Project. In each of these projects ideas were generated in the field, tested and gradually shaped into a project design. Preliminary outlines of the project design were prepared and circulated to help ensure a consensus on important design features. In Niger, the outline of the proposed design was published on the front page of the national newspaper, and frequent radio broadcasts reported on the progress of the design team. In Ethiopia and Tanzania - VD, national officials fully accepted the project design that emerged from the working level, which resulted in a high commitment to the projects. The Regional Commissioner responsible for implementing the Tanzania Village Development Project came to Washington for the project review and articulately argued for the project. In Tanzania - FT and Niger, however, problems were encountered because of differences regarding the project approach and project management arrangements.

Mixed Experience with Collaboration

The degree of collaboration and the levels where it took place differed significantly in the twelve design efforts. The nature of the collaboration was found to have a direct effect on the degree of commitment to the project obtained from host country implementing agencies and key officials. These relationships are shown in Table 2.3.

In four cases (Afghanistan, Chile, Colombia and Upper Volta - OP), the implementing responsibility lay directly with a national agency. The Chile Farm Management Project and Upper Volta Oncho Project are examples of close agreement between the design team and host country government officials on the development problem to be addressed and on the development approach to be used.

In direct contrast is the Colombia Small Farmer Development Project where the timetable for project preparation negated meaningful collaboration on the

TABLE 2.3

HOST COUNTRY COLLABORATION

Project	Project-(Working) Level Collaboration	Project-Level Influence on Design	National-Level Collaboration	National-Level Influence on Design	Commitment of Implementing Agency to Project As Designed
Afghanistan [1]	-	-	3	1	1
Chile [1]	-	-	5	5	5
Colombia [1]	-	-	1	1	1
Ethiopia	5	5	5	1	5[3]
Ghana	1	1	1	1	1
Haiti (DAI design) [2]	-	-	None	None	1
Niger (DAI design)	5	3	5	1	3
Tanzania - FT	5	5	1	1	1
Tanzania - VD	5	5	1	1	5
Upper Volta - OP [1]	-	-	5	5	5
Upper Volta - WP	3	1	1	1	3
Zaire	3	1	5	3	3

Code: High = 5; Medium = 3; Low = 1; (-)=not applicable since collaboration was at national level.

[1] Project and National Levels coincide.

[2] Project management arrangements were undetermined.

[3] The commitment of the national-level implementing agency was high.

part of the implementing agency (although Colombians outside the decisionmaking structure participated). This resulted in a lack of commitment to the project by the implementing agency, which became apparent during the implementation phase. While an attempt was made to generate an effective collaborative effort in Afghanistan, there were serious disagreements between the implementing agency and the design team about project implementation arrangements.[8]

In some cases design teams had reservations about the selection or capabilities of designated implementing agencies. In the Haiti Integrated Agricultural Project, field-testing revealed several alternatives for the selection of the implementing agency, ranging from a national agency to a private voluntary organization. There were serious questions about the capabilities of the national agency to interact effectively with the local population. Developing the project with this agency would have implied a commitment to implement through it. Similar situations appeared at the project level in the Zaire North Shaba Project and in the Upper Volta Women's Project.

The design of the Upper Volta Women's Project reflects another problem in developing meaningful collaboration. The only individual with effective decisionmaking responsibility was the Minister of Rural Development, who was burdened with many national concerns, making frequent interaction almost impossible. This was equally true in Afghanistan, Chile and Colombia.

The benefits derived from having local government officials involved in the design process varied significantly among the projects. In Zaire, local officials were seen as policing agents and tax collectors, so a conscious decision was made to exclude them from visits to villages. On the other hand, local officials in Upper Volta normally have training in *animation* (motivation) techniques; they respect the knowledge held by farmers, and thus were facilitators in the design process. Although local officials in Ethiopia traveled and worked with the design team for three weeks, they had business beyond the project design to conduct that frequently interfered with their design roles.

Conclusions Concerning Collaboration

Participation in the twelve design exercises has provided a number of valuable conclusions.

First, meaningful collaboration, especially at the local level, cannot be accomplished in rapid, one- or two-day excursions to the field. Where such fleeting visits took place (e.g., Niger), important information was missed, in particular an assessment of local organizational capabilities. Relatively intensive exposure to the project area is needed (perhaps three or four weeks, depending on the size of the area) so that initial suspicions are overcome and data can be checked and rechecked. Ideally, the design team should stay overnight in local communities at least part of the time, so that informal discussions can take place.

The fact that collaboration tends to generate enthusiasm for a project was found to have both positive and negative dimensions. There is a very real possiblity that a project will get stalled in the approval process; when this happens, the result is an erosion of popular support, official commitment to the project, and an apparent vindication of the view that outsiders cannot be trusted.[9]

A closely related point is that local collaboration may result in a strong commitment to a project by future staff members and by the local population, but this work will be in vain if national-level decisionmakers have different views about what the project should look like. In the Tanzania Farmer Training Project, for example, there was a conflict between local and national views over the type of training program required for the project; predictably, the national viewpoint prevailed. Thus, the strength of the link between local and national officials has to be assessed when determining the strategy for collaboration.

National officials with decisionmaking responsibilities rarely have the time to become deeply involved in the design process. The principal avenues for collaboration are periodic formal meetings and (often more important) informal discussions over a beer. When a lower-level official has direct access to the key decisionmaker, he can be a useful intermediary. If not, the chances that a fully agreed-upon project will emerge are almost nil. Whatever the opportunity for collaboration, it is necessary for key decisionmakers to be involved at each stage of the design process. One mechanism for ensuring this is to furnish them outlines, each including critical decisions and options and developing in more detail the project design.

A final lesson concerns agreement on project strategy. Adopting a process approach to project development may pose difficulties for host country officials. First, the process approach suggests that answers to the problem of inducing small farmer behavior change in a particular area have not been found. This challenges the programs that have already been developed by host country and foreign donor agencies. Second, the process approach calls for information gathering, testing of the alternatives generated, and then action and replication. Many host country officials are under significant pressures to produce results in a short time frame. This means that a significant amount of time may be necessary in the beginning just to get agreement on project strategy before proceeding to the details of project content.

These lessons and considerations argue strongly for close and creative collaboration in the design process, as well as in project implementation. While this knowledge is held by most AID staff, the bureaucratic demands of obligating funds still cause some designs, as in this sample, to be formulated around a table in USAID offices. The results are quick, clean and efficient but will not reflect host country thinking nor generate a strong host country commitment to implement the project as designed. The Project Paper so designed will bear little relationship to the project that is finally implemented. Hindsight reinforces the notion that involvement and participation are as important in retaining the commitment of host country decisionmakers, as they are in gaining the cooperation of small farmers.

NOTES

1 The project design in Afghanistan was DAI's responsibility; in Haiti it was not.

2 Defining critical data requirements and then satisfying them during a period of intensive design remains an art form that is given little assistance by the various AID handbooks. DAI generated an outline of information requirements for area development, which was used in four projects. It was further refined and submitted with the draft report, but withheld from the final report because it was prescriptive and not in consonance with the rest of the study. A manual for project design based on these data requirements has been prepared for the Agency.

3 Before DAI involvement with the project, Chilean professionals were given a copy of AID's Project Paper guidelines without

direction. The end result was a 300-page document covering the history of agrarian reform in Chile, but scarcely addressing the issues of small farmer development (credit, technology, etc.) or the questions of project structure and organization.

[4] The complexity of closed Afghan rural society suggests that few answers are currently available on vital "how to" questions. This is particularly true when a major question is how to enter the local community by means other than through the traditional leadership. See David D. Gow, "Data Gathering for Project Design: The Afghan Experience," Development Alternatives, Inc., internal paper, December 1976.

[5] For a more extensive explanation of analysis techniques see Development Alternatives, Inc., *Information for Decisionmaking in Rural Development* (two volumes), prepared for the Office of Rural Development and Development Administration, AID, May 22, 1978.

[6] Based on a larger sample, the reaction of Missions in Africa to the review/approval process was obtained. The study concluded that a significant proportion of all expenses were unnecessary and undertaken solely to get projects approved. *Project Development in East and Southern Africa,* op. cit.

[7] Frequently it was found that consultative meetings with officials and potential beneficiaries needed to be conducted separately in order to ensure that the latter would state their views openly.

[8] See Chapters 4 and 8 for further discussion of the organizational arrangements for project implementation.

[9] The effect on implementation of delays in the review/approval process is discussed further in Chapters 3 and 9.

3
The Review/Approval Process

INTRODUCTION

This chapter will describe and analyze what happened to the twelve projects as they moved through the AID review/approval process. More specifically, the analysis is intended to:

- Identify the major sources of delay affecting the movement of projects through the system;
- Explain the causes of these delays; and
- Draw some preliminary conclusions regarding the way the system functioned as the twelve projects moved through it.[1]

The issues can best be approached through an examination of the chronology of the twelve projects. Table 3.1 presents this chronology and reveals an uneven pattern in the intervals between critical decisions in the review/approval process. The small size of the sample restricts the latitude for generalizations about this pattern, and the analysis depends on in-depth study of the projects within the set. Even so, it is possible to discern persistent problems within the system that require resolution.

Four of the projects (Chile, Colombia, Haiti and Zaire) are distinguished by the relative smoothness of their passage through the system. No significant objections were raised in AID/Washington to the designs of these projects, whereas each of the remaining eight was challenged on at least one major point, leading to substantial delay in approval.

TABLE 3.1

CHRONOLOGY OF REVIEW/APPROVAL ACTIONS

	Document Submitted	Document Approved	Time Taken	Time to Next Document
Afghanistan Integrated Rural Development Project				
PID	-	-	-	-
Rural Works PP	1/22/75	-	-	23 mos.
DAI Study	11/28/76	-	-	2 mos.
PP Amendment 1	1/29/77	-	-	5 mos.
PP Amendment 2	6/14/77	8/26/77	2 mos.	
Project Agreement		9/18/77	1 mo.	
Chile Farm Management Project				
IRR	2/75	-	-	15 mos.
Interim Report	5/3/76	7/8/76	2 mos.	10 mos.
PP	5/31/77	6/77	1 mos.	-
Colombia Small Farmer Development Project				
IRR	1975	4/29/75	-	8 mos.
PP	12/5/75	12/30/75	25 days	6 mos.
Loan Agreement	-	6/14/76	-	-
Ethiopia Rehabilitation Project				
PID	6/6/76	6/76	-	6 mos.
PRP	12/6/76	4/77	4 mos.	-
Mini-PP	4/13/77	7/11/77	3 mos.	-
Ghana District Development Project				
PID	7/3/75	9/27/75	2 mos.	8 mos.
PRP 1	5/28/76	-	-	4 mos.
PRP 2	9/3/76	-	-	7 mos.
PP	4/21/77	6/27/77	2 mos.	1 mo.
Grant Agreement	-	7/77	-	-
Haiti Integrated Agricultural Project				
PID	8/75	-	-	4 mos.
DAI Paper	12/75	-	-	7 mos.
PP 1	7/29/76	-	-	2 mos
PP 2	9/22/76	9/27/76	5 days	7 mos.
Loan Agreement	-	4/27/77		

TABLE 3.1 (Continued)

	Document Submitted	Document Approved	Time Taken	Time to Next Document
Niger Department Development Project				
PID	-	6/75	-	6 mos.
PRP	12/75	1/8/76	1 mo.	7 mos.
PP 1	8/76	-	-	7 mos.
PP 2	3/4/77	5/25/77	2 mos.	3 mos.
Project Agreement	-	8/29/77	-	-
Tanzania Farmer Training Project				
PID	-	-	-	-
PRP 1	1/75	-	-	9 mos.
PRP 2	10/24/75	12/10/75	2 mos.	3 mos.
PP	3/29/76	8/8/77	16 mos.	1 mo.
Project Agreement	-	9/13/77	-	-
Tanzania Village Development Project				
PID	11/30/76	3/9/77	3 mos.	4 mos.
PP 1	7/77	-	-	9 mos.
PP 2	4/15/78	7/7/78	3 mos.	-
Upper Volta Oncho Project				
PID	1975	10/17/75	-	1 mo.
PRP	11/20/75	12/17/75	1 mo.	6 mos.
PP	6/28/76	9/7/77	15 mos.	-
Upper Volta Women's Project				
PID	5/75	6/75	1 mo.	6 mos.
PRP	12/12/75	2/19/76	2 mos.	4 mos.
PP 1	6/28/76	-	-	7 mos.
PP 2	1/77	3/11/77	2 mos.	6 mos.
Grant Agreement	-	9/30/77	-	-
Zaire North Shaba Project				
PID	12/12/74	-	-	16 mos.
PRP	3/76	5/10/76	2 mos.	4 mos.
PP	9/17/76	9/30/76	13 days	0
Project Agreement	-	9/30/76		

Is it fair to conclude, on this basis, that the four projects that were approved relatively quickly were the best designed and destined to be the easiest to implement? This judgment would mean that the existing system works well for well designed projects. Closer examination suggests that this is not necessarily true: the fate of the four projects is better interpreted with reference to procedural differences between the Latin America and Africa Bureaus. The case of Zaire is an exception; it suggests that greater "efficiency" can be achieved in the closing days of the fiscal year.[2]

Reflections on the review/approval system will be examined in Chapter 9. In the discussion that follows, attention is focused on the principal sources of delay for the eight remaining projects. Table 3.2 shows the eight projects affected in relation to six major problem areas. Each of the problem areas is subjected to detailed analysis in the remainder of this chapter.

THE ADEQUATE PLANNING REQUIREMENT[3]

One of the six areas that has been a source of significant delay in the project review and approval process concerns Congressional legislation. Section 611(a)(1) of the Foreign Assistance Act states that:

> (a) No agreement or grant which constitutes an obligation of the United States Government in excess of $100,000...shall be made for any assistance....
>
> (1) if such agreement or grant requires substantial technical or financial planning, until engineering, financial, and other plans necessary to carry out such assistance, and a reasonably firm estimate of the cost to the United States Government of providing such assistance, have been completed....[4]

In essence, this provision requires adequate planning before funds are obligated.

The source of this legislation was the Mutual Security Act of 1958, which was an attempt to overcome the delays in negotiating and planning projects with foreign governments, and at the same time

TABLE 3.2

SOURCES OF DELAY IN THE REVIEW/APPROVAL PROCESS

Project	Adequate Planning Requirement	Procedural Uncer-tainties	Environ-mental Review	Personnel Qualifi-cations	Conflict Over Design Methods	Other Reasons
Afghanistan					X	
Ethiopia		X	X			X[a]
Ghana	X	X				X[b]
Niger	X	X	X		X	
Tanzania - FT				X		
Tanzania - VD	X		X	X		
Upper Volta - OP	X	X				X[c]
Upper Volta - WP	X	X				

a Human rights considerations.

b International political incident.

c Health certification requirement.

provide adequate planning for projects prior to the obligation of funds. The need was reflected in a report of the House Foreign Affairs Committee, which stated:

> [F]unds are obligated, and consequently may be carried forward from year to year until expended, on the basis of an agreement with a foreign government even though such agreement is not supported by construction or procurement contracts. The result is that funds are appropriated by the Congress to build factories and for other projects 2 or 3 years, in a number of cases, before the engineering plans...are completed.[5]

The original legislative concern, to ensure that funds not be "squirreled away" for future projects, was not an issue in any of the projects under review. Instead, discussions focused on the degree of planning that was "adequate" to satisfy the legislation. The legislation is vague and the General Counsel has not provided project designers with clear guidelines on how this legislation is to be interpreted. The result is that AID/Washington has maintained considerable discretionary power to interpret Section 611(a)(1) as it chooses.

During an interview, a representative of the Africa Section of the General Counsel's Office was asked why regulations concerning the legislation were not developed for designers. The response was first that there were insufficient resources to undertake the job, and second that any such regulations would risk being interpreted literally and result in a violation of the spirit of the law, since general guidelines do not fit all situations. Any interpretation would yield the same result as if no regulations existed.

In the Latin America Bureau, the project design system operates with a clear idea of how the section will be interpreted and how to write a project design that will satisfy the General Counsel. In the past, Africa Bureau project designers have had little clear idea either of how the section will be interpreted, or of how to write a project that will satisfy the General Counsel. Moreover, the field and AID/Washington disagree on the meaning of Section 611(a)(1).

Specific Problems Under 611(a)(1)

Of the twelve projects reviewed, six encountered substantial delays in the review process.[6] In each case the delays resulted from the omission of detailed specifications for the use of project funds, although general criteria for obligating the funds were presented. In the process approach to project design, only a general criterion could be provided; specific criteria would become available as the project evolved. As of the end of May 1978, all projects except Tanzania - VD had been approved, and Section 611(a)(1) had been satisfied in a variety of ways.[7]

The easiest case, where no substantial delays were encountered, was Ethiopia. Here, authority was transferred from AID/Washington to the Mission Director as part of the new Agency regulations that authorized a Mission Director to "approve projects costing $500,000 or less."[8] While this did not eliminate the obligation to satisfy the criteria of Section 611(a)(1), it did delegate the authority to the Mission.[9] Since implementation of the planning phase is just beginning, it is not yet known how this will be managed.[10]

In the Ghana project, a district development and experimental fund of $160,000 was included in the pre-implementation phase. While the project has been approved, these funds can not be obligated until after the Mission has submitted "adequate" plans for the proposed activities.

The Niger project was delayed on two separate planning issues. First, to assure that adequate planning would be done on the rural works component of the project, AID/Washington required through the General Counsel that a representative from REDSO/WA review and certify all plans. The second, more complicated issue concerned an "experimental fund." This was resolved by using an intermediary credit institution. By this institutionalization of credit, the fund was not only kept in the project design, but actually increased sevenfold from the first PP design (which had been rejected for non-compliance with Section 611[a][1], among other reasons). The only stipulation for the allocation of these funds was that "a thorough study of existing credit mechanisms" be undertaken and submitted to AID/Washington for approval.

Satisfaction of Section 611(a)(1) came for both Upper Volta projects only after lengthy and heated debate between the Mission and AID/Washington. At one point, the Mission Director argued that it was impossible to locate, design and cost microprojects and that such an attempt would defeat the project purpose. It was his opinion that the current interpretation of this legislation by AID/Washington was blocking projects, as well as being contrary to the intention of Congress. He recommended amending the legislation.[11]

In both projects, Section 611(a)(1) was satisfied by adding Conditions Precedent to the Grant Agreements, specifying the criteria for obligating monies from the fund.[12] They included credit eligibility criteria, interest rates and repayment terms, an accounting and information system, and feasibility studies on recommended activities.

The Haiti project stands in marked contrast to the African projects on the subject of 611(a)(1). All problems with interpretation of 611(a)(1) were avoided by inserting a Condition Precedent requiring adequate planning for credit prior to the disbursement of funds for this component. Funds for the specialist to satisfy the planning requirements were then included in the Project Paper.

As with the Niger project, the Tanzania Village Development Project originally failed to meet the criteria of Section 611(a)(1) on the issue of adequate planning for the rural works component of the project. Subsequently adequate planning requirements were broadened to other components of the project. The status of the project evolved as follows:

- During the Executive Committee Project Review (ECPR) of September 28, 1977, the 611(a)(1) issue revolved around adequate planning for rural works projects. As a result criteria were developed for meeting the requirements for the construction of roads and village water and irrigation systems; these included: (a) the specification of design standards for the roads and water and irrigation systems; (b) cost estimates based upon the standards specified; and (c) criteria for selection of construction sites. Engineers from REDSO and AID/Washington were asked to undertake the data collection necessary to meet these criteria.

- After the ECPR meeting, concern developed in AID/Washington that other components of the project -- namely the agricultural production and other economic activities -- had not met the requirements for adequate planning. AID/Washington gave the USAID Mission in Tanzania several alternatives for meeting 611(a)(1). The first was to prepare and cost a list of alternative agricultural production activities from which the villages would ultimately choose. The list could be made relatively flexible by specifying criteria for additional activities that would be added to it. As an alternative, work plans specifying village production activities could be submitted to USAID for review as they were identified, permitting funds to be obligated only after the plans were approved by the Mission Director.

In the case of other economic activities (primarily the identification, production and dissemination of appropriate technology), Project Development Support funds would be obligated for an appropriate technology feasibility study. To satisfy 611(a)(1) requirements, it was suggested: (a) that the feasibility study could provide sufficient information to settle on alternative activities that would be undertaken (similar to the "list" concept prepared for the agricultural production activities); or (b) that funds would be obligated as activities were identified in the work plans and approved by the Mission.

- From November 1977 to January 1978 the data collection for the rural works components of the project was carried out by road engineers from REDSO and a water hydrologist from AID/Washington. In February one member of the original DAI PP design team, along with a person from AID/Washington and another from the REDSO legal staff, returned to Tanzania to assist the Mission in rewriting the PP, incorporating the road and water data. In the case of agricultural and other economic activities, the Mission chose to have work plans submitted to the Mission for the Directors' approval as these activities were identified.

All of this added up to a lengthy, expensive delay in project implementation. The result was an increase from 41.4 person-weeks to carry out the original PP design to a total of 63.4 (giving this project the highest level of resources committed for design of the twelve projects under review)[13] and a greatly expanded Project Paper (three volumes).[14] At the same time, total AID grant projections for the project changed from $15.66 million in the first PP to $14.59 in the revised version!

The experience with the project reinforces the suggestion that has already been made that there has been no coherent policy in the Africa Bureau to handle the "adequate planning" requirement. Because of the energy expended in the project in defining how 611(a)(1) could be dealt with -- particularly the important input made by the legal staff from REDSO -- it might provide a model for subsequent projects. Unfortunately solutions to the 611(a)(1) issue have to a large degree reflected the points of view of the particular AID staff involved with a project, which reduces the likelihood of a model being adopted.

General Conclusions Under 611(a)(1)

In reviewing the problems encountered by these six projects in satisfying the criteria of Section 611(a)(1), it becomes clear that a fundamental tenet of the process approach -- that it is impossible to determine in advance all project activities that may be appropriate -- is in conflict with the Africa Bureau's interpretation of the advance planning requirement of the legislation. There are several dimensions to this problem. First, there is the question of what existing procedures might be employed to satisfy the adequate planning requirement. Second, there is the question of when, in the review/approval process, the requirements must be satisfied. Finally, there is the question of who has the authority to determine whether the requirement has been satisfied. Each of these issues is discussed below.

Existing Procedural Vehicles to Satisfy 611(a)(1)

There are several ways to deal with the problem and still satisfy the approving offices within AID/Washington who rely heavily on the General Counsel. One is to modify the project objective to include the institutionalization of credit. Using this approach, it is not necessary to specify in detail how the funds will be used. However, considerable information must be included about the institution: interest and repayment rates, accounting system and so forth.

A second way to satisfy the General Counsel is to provide, to the extent possible, specific details of the ways in which project funds will be used. This might be done by defining a limited number of subprojects, costing them in detail, and specifying a ceiling limit for the total mix of activities (subprojects) that would receive assistance. For those subprojects for which detailed costing cannot be done, criteria could be established for meeting the adequate planning requirements and the Mission Director could be given the authority to obligate funds when they are met. The Tanzania - VD project has moved in this direction.

A third method, which may only work in Latin America, is to designate a project as a "research" undertaking, which seemed to satisfy the requirements of 611(a)(1) in the Colombia Small Farmer Development Project.

Timing

Four Africa projects (Ghana, the two Upper Volta projects and Niger) incurred long delays in project approval as AID/Washington and the Missions argued over what it took to satisfy Section 611(a)(1). These issues were not resolved. Instead, the projects were approved with stipulations that adequate planning would be carried out prior to obligation of funds for the particular project component in question.

The conflicts on this subject in the Africa Bureau stand in marked contrast to what happened with the Haiti project. In that case, the Latin America Bureau accepted from the outset that adequate planning for the credit component could take place after project approval. Indeed, part of the funds obligated for the project were to carry out the required planning work.

The Africa Bureau's position appears to be inconsistent. Either it should have adopted the general approach used by the Latin America Bureau from the outset and agreed that adequate planning could be carried out after the project was approved, or it should have consistently required adequate planning prior to project approval. Instead, project approvals were delayed on grounds that adequate planning had to be completed first, and finally, after considerable argument and delay, approvals were given with the stipulation that the planning would be done later. This outcome can be viewed as a positive result of a learning process if it is applied consistently to future project proposals.

Delegation of Authority

In Ethiopia and Tanzania, authority to satisfy the 611(a)(1) requirements was delegated to the Mission Director. This did not reduce the planning requirements; it merely made them the Mission Director's responsibility.

Results of delegating the responsibility for the satisfaction of the 611(a)(1) requirements in the four Africa projects are not yet clear. However, it is reasonable to assume that this will mean a partial delegation to the field missions of the authority to satisfy the section.

Conclusions

In the sample reviewed, the adequate planning requirement has caused long delays in the approval of projects designed with an evolutionary approach. The interpretation of the 611(a)(1) requirements may be conceptually consistent within regional bureaus, but it provides the greatest obstacle to project design and approval (of all the different potentials for "delay" encountered) in the Africa Bureau. The adequate planning requirement hinders the attempts of AID to implement the "New Directions" mandate. Recommendations to overcome these problems are set forth in Chapter 10.

PROCEDURAL UNCERTAINTIES

In recent years, a number of changes have been made in AID review/approval procedures. It is understandable, therefore, that some misunderstandings arise, and problems of a strictly procedural nature develop, because AID personnel are not thoroughly conversant with specific changes. Nevertheless, there is evidence that delays are not always due to such misunderstandings and/or procedural causes. When there is general agreement among the principal actors that a project should be approved, the possibility that it may nevertheless be "trapped" in the review/approval system is cause for urgent concern.

The Ghana project is an example of this phenomenon, for while it did not encounter serious objections from any quarters within AID/Washington, it ran afoul of procedural delays that stalled implementation for nearly two years. The following excerpts from the project's chronology illustrate how its momentum was slowed and eventually halted:

- On September 27, 1975, a cable from AID/Washington to USAID/Accra indicated that the PID had been approved by the Executive Committee for Project Review. Among other things, the Executive Committee instructed the Mission to justify, in the PRP, U.S. support for grant funding of housing, since this cost was usually borne by the host country government. More than a year later (October 8, 1976), a desk officer indicated that, while no one in AID opposed the project, they were having problems figuring out how to house a person in the chosen district, since there was no money in the first phase of the project for a house.

- At the July 1976 annual budget submission review meeting, it was decided that the fiscal year portion of the rural development loan should be incorporated into the PRP. This decision was made because it was not possible for USAID/Accra to discuss the rural development resource loan with the Ghanaians until Secretary of State Kissinger had made his final decision on the Ghana program. This delay meant that there would not be time to include the loan component in the FY 1978 Congressional budgetary presentation. The second PRP was submitted in September 1976 and reviewed by the Project Committee on October 15, 1976. The committee endorsed the grant portion of the project, but the newly included loan element of five million dollars was not accepted by either the Bureau for Program and Policy Coordination (PPC) or the General Counsel on grounds that it might be in violation of Section 611(a)(1). It was decided to send the PRP back to USAID/Accra and to reconvene the Project Committee review meeting to decide on the approval of the PRP with or without the loan. In early December, the Executive Committee approved the PRP with the condition that the loan portion be investigated and the PRP be resubmitted by March or April of 1977.

- In early March 1977, the General Counsel ruled that the activities planned no longer constituted a design exercise and that, consequently, the Government of Ghana must contribute twenty-five percent of the total project costs. Just how this provision was to be met was the subject of considerable discussion in AID/Washington memos; yet in other AID projects this criterion usually has not proved too difficult to satisfy.

- On May 24, 1977, a cable came in to AID/Washington from the Mission indicating "further technical difficulties with the funding and allotments."

- The project implementation RFP finally was published in the *Commerce Business Daily* on October 25, 1977, more than two years after the approval of the PID. The AID contracts office had been trying to obtain a satisfactory PIO/T and scope of work from the Mission, for preparation of the RFP, nine months earlier, in January 1977.

The striking thing about the fate of the Ghana project within the review/approval process is that the delays were due neither to major disagreements nor to conflicting interpretations of marginal issues. This project enjoyed the general support of all parties concerned with moving it through to approval and implementation. However ambiguous AID procedures and interpretations almost killed it.

A stronger indication that procedures are ignored or inadequately understood in certain parts of AID/Washington emerges from the case history for the two Upper Volta projects, which were reviewed during a period of reorganization in the Africa Bureau. In neither case was the General Counsel invited to the Project Review Committee meeting. The upshot of this bureaucratic error was that the meetings had to be reconvened after considerable time had elapsed, delaying approval of both projects.

Many of the procedural problems appear to revolve around the role of Project Review Committees within the Africa Bureau. In the Latin America Bureau, a lower-level group prepares an issues paper to be considered by the Development Assistance Executive Committee. In the Africa Bureau, the Project Review Committee has the authority to review and recommend project approval.[15] Projects with issues that cannot be resolved by consensus in the Project Review Committees, or that are in excess of ten million dollars, must be referred to a Senior Review Committee.

The case of the Niger project raises doubts about the effectiveness of a two-tiered committee system. When the final PP was presented, the lower-level committee questioned the underlying philosophy of the project, specifically asking whether it was primarily an "experimental" effort or an "action" project. The Mission Director,[16] who had not attended this meeting, requested a second one, which was held in November 1976. The outcome of the second meeting was an instruction to the Mission Director to revise the Project Paper. This was done, and on March 18, 1977, the Project Review Committee met again with the Mission Director in attendance. When full agreement could not be reached in this session, an issues paper was prepared for the Executive Committee.

The issues paper made it very clear that the Project Review Committee remained dissatisfied with the revised PP, and raised three particular questions that had to be resolved:

- Did the project represent a testing and design phase of a multi-phased, integrated rural development project?

- Was the project adequately structured to provide the project managers with the information they would need to evaluate and modify the individual project elements?

- Was this the project that AID/Washington had requested, in view of original budgeting proposals that now seemed to have been altered significantly, with spending continued for a year beyond the original limit?

These questions were not peripheral, but were basic to the entire assessment of the project. Despite fundamental problems with these basic issues at the lower level, the Executive Committee decided at its meeting of April 14, 1977, to approve the project.

The Niger experience calls into serious question the appropriateness of dividing project review activity between two levels since the resolution of issues took an inordinate amount of time. Between December 1975, when the PP was first submitted, and April 1977, it appears that no real progress was made in resolving the principal substantive issues. The Project Review Committee was strongly opposed to an "action" project. The Executive Committee sided with the Mission Director in favor of having an "action" project.

On the basis of this observation, it is worth asking what purpose is served by this division of authority. A committee reviewing the work of the Africa Bureau recently recommended that current review procedures be abolished. They commented:

> ...people feel obliged to justify their existence at committee meetings by talking and defending positions, and such meetings are an invitation to confrontation rather than resolution of problems. If the review committees were abolished, field representatives, accompanied by the Desk, would be responsible for obtaining necessary clearances and making appropriate changes.[17]

The utility of this suggestion is shown in Chapter 9, along with other reflections on the review/approval process.

ENVIRONMENTAL REVIEW

In June 1976 new procedures were introduced into the AID project review system "to ensure that environmental factors and values are integrated into the decisionmaking process and to assign responsibility within the Agency for assessing the environmental impacts of AID's actions."[18] Currently, the Agency is still grappling with the problem of implementing the procedures in a meaningful way. For three of the projects (Ethiopia, Niger, and Tanzania - VD), environmental issues were raised in the course of the review process. The handling of these issues indicates that the guidelines for effecting the new procedures are not fully understood in all quarters.

Under the new requirements, the environmental office in each AID/Washington regional bureau must make a recommendation, based on an Initial Environmental Examination (IEE) attached to the PID, about whether any environmental consequences are likely to arise from a particular project. This recommendation forms the basis of a decision regarding the need for further consideration of environmental issues. If a "negative determination" is made, signifying that the project is not likely to have significant effects on the environment, no further consideration is required.

If the review of the PID indicates that the likelihood of environmental impact appears strong, steps will be taken to recruit an environmentalist for the completion of a more extensive study in the form of an Environmental Assessment (EA) or an Environmental Impact Statement (EIS). The latter is a highly specific document that must be written in a format developed by the United States Environmental Protection Agency. To date, the Africa Bureau has completed two EAs, with five more in process. Only one EIS has been prepared, which dealt with overall AID policy on the use of pesticides.

Two issues came up during the course of project review for the Ethiopia, Tanzania - VD, and Niger projects, regarding measurement of environmental impact. These were:

- When should the environmental examination be done?

- How many environmental examinations are needed?

The problem posed by the first question is similar to that posed by the Section 611(a)(1) requirements for projects following an evolutionary approach. Given the nature of this approach, it is frequently much more difficult to make a judgment at the time of project approval regarding probable environmental effects, than with a conventional project whose design constitutes a highly specific blueprint for proposed activities. In both Niger and Tanzania - VD, issues papers were prepared within AID/Washington calling for preparation of detailed environmental examinations. Both projects had been designed to include an initial phase of field-testing to identify activities for subsequent phases.

As far as the second question is concerned, there appears to be some doubt about whether separate environmental examinations are required for each project activity. Here again the inclusion of a provision for field-testing, often involving micro-projects to be supported with as little as $500 from project funds, raises potentially serious questions. In the Ethiopia project, doubts about the procedural requirements for evaluating activities at the sub-project level were reflected in cable traffic between the Mission and AID/Washington. The Mission Director wrote that:

> ...separate IEE [for] each sub-project would mean under present rules AA/AFR approval as many as 25 IEE's for this project in period 4-8 months. [The] chain [of] events [for] each IEE from peasant association, provincial development committee, provincial administrator, Minister [of] Interior or RRC/USAID, AFR-DR, and AA-AFR indicates impracticability of such procedure.[19]

For both questions, delegation of authority to the Mission would seem to be the best way to obtain sound answers. Long delays in project approval would appear to be inappropriate when the broader environmental questions are imponderable. On the other hand, funds for specific activities should not be disbursed until it can be demonstrated that what is proposed will not have adverse environmental effects. The environmental staff in AID/Washington is currently very small; for example, the Africa Bureau has only two staffers to review IEEs for about 100 projects per year. Even if there were latitude for a significant buildup in staff, it is doubtful that it would be cost-effective to involve AID/Washington directly in all of the judgments required by activities in projects using the process approach. Mission Directors, by contrast, can be expected to follow project development sufficiently closely to make environmental judgments as they are required.

QUALIFICATIONS OF TECHNICAL ASSISTANCE PERSONNEL

In both of the Tanzania projects, a fundamental question arose regarding the type of background and experience required of the individuals to be recruited for project implementation. This issue has potential bearing on all of the projects. The main obstacle to its resolution is a sharp difference of opinion regarding the most effective methods of communicating with a target population of small farmers.

All of the twelve projects concerned rural development and, in one way or another, all of them aimed at increasing agricultural production and income. In the latter regard, the question posed during the review process for both Tanzania projects was whether project goals could be achieved more efficiently and rapidly by recruiting individuals with primarily agricultural backgrounds.[20]

For rural development projects specifically focusing on small farmer populations, the process approach requires above all that the implementing team be able to interact in both a learning and a teaching capacity with small farmers. There is clearly a need for various technical capacities to be represented on the implementation team. Regrettably, though, no single traditional discipline trains individuals to implement the process approach. It becomes necessary therefore to recruit a proper mix of specialist and generalist skills for the teams that carry out such projects in the field.

Both Tanzania projects incorporated the process approach, and their designs called for implementation teams with a broader mix of skills than purely agricultural and technical specialties. In the final PP for the Farmer Training Project, however, a predominant capability waiver was requested -- at the initiative of the Tanzania AID Mission -- to procure the exclusive services of the West Virginia University/North Carolina Agricultural and Technical State University Consortium. This request encountered strenuous objections from the General Counsel, AID/Washington. On January 7, 1977, the General Counsel concluded that the PP did not adequately justify the request for the waiver. On the contrary, he pointed out, the project called for personnel skilled in recruitment, training and evaluation, with expertise in organizational development, and knowledgeable and experienced in the dynamics of small farmer production. The General Counsel concluded: "to propose seeking a predominant capability waiver for an institution so lacking in the basic skills necessary to carry out the project reveals a serious lack of concern or knowledge of basic U.S. contracting principles."[21]

During the review of the Tanzania Village Development PP, agricultural specialists within AID/Washington advocated that the project be implemented by technical assistance personnel with formal agricultural training. The original design proposed that technical assistance be provided by rural development specialists. The outcome of this challenge is still not determined, but will likely be something of a compromise, including the addition of an agricultural specialist position and the provision that the rural development specialists have some agricultural training or experience. The job descriptions of the technical assistance staff were rewritten to include the stricter qualifications.[22]

In the Tanzania Farmer Training Project, these objections to the skills and specialty composition of the project team came at a very late stage in the review/approval process. The objections represented an attempt to return the project to its "first principles," reversing Mission-induced modifications. The fact that the "first principles" were part and parcel of the process approach is secondary and does not imply a judgment that the review system functioned adequately. More important is the evidence that mechanisms exist that can substantially delay approval and implementation of projects on specific technical grounds, after design completion. The material question, then, is whether those mechanisms serve any useful purpose. They relate to a more general issue, namely, the diffusion of authority within the review/approval system, and its consequences for projects that must move through the system. An attempt to resolve that general issue is made in the reflective discussion of the approval system in Chapter 9.

CONFLICTS OVER DESIGN METHODOLOGY

Among the twelve projects reviewed in this report, the Afghanistan project encountered the greatest resistance within the AID review/approval system. That resistance was ultimately strong enough to forestall approval, on the grounds that the project design methodology was technically inadequate. This position was maintained by the Office of Technical Support of the Near East Bureau (NE/TECH) in AID/Washington, whose views eventually prevailed over those of the Mission and the original design team. Since NE/TECH was kind enough to offer comments on the draft version of this report, an attempt will be made to highlight the main points at issue in the case.

Having previously completed an evaluation of the Afghanistan Rural Works Project, DAI was asked, as a follow-on, to design an integrated rural development (IRD) project that was to become an amendment to the Rural Works Project. It was possible to carry out an extensive design effort, and findings from observations and surveys in the field indicated that an evolutionary, process-oriented approach was needed.

In this instance, unlike others where DAI staff actually helped to write Project Papers, a study was produced outlining the design for a pilot district development project. It did not meet all PP format requirements and did not specify the implementation arrangements (since the latter had not been agreed upon prior to the departure of the design team). The Mission used this study in preparing an amended Rural Works PP, in which support for IRD activities in Mohammad Agha District was one of three components. DAI also spent some time at AID/Washington going over the proposal in an attempt to clarify and expand upon some of the issues raised by the field report and the Project Paper.

The fundamental premise of the design was that exploratory work had to be done to determine how to intervene in local Afghan communities, and that when this determination was made, field-testing of possible interventions could be undertaken within those communities. It was argued that the knowledge base in Afghanistan was so weak that project activities and outputs could not be specified in elaborate detail during the design phase.

Over the course of the next six months, a sustained and ultimately successful challenge to the project was mounted by NE/TECH. On May 11, 1977, the Mission capitulated to what is assumed was AID/Washington's implicit rejection of the project and wrote a second PP amendment, which eliminated the IRD as designed by DAI and originally put forward by the Mission. In its place was a single planning advisor who was to decide, in effect, what to do next.

The key issues and the nature of the principal objections raised turned on NE/TECH's view that the DAI study and the resulting amended PP had these weaknesses:

- Insufficient information on local institutions, economic relationships, resource distribution and use, etc., to furnish a realistic guide for an AID-supported project;

- Incorrect "experimental" methodology, which had to be corrected by the selection of both a different district for the project, and a second, "control" district, and a design to accommodate specifications appropriate in classical "experiments"; and

- Inappropriate design components, including over-ambitious technical assistance, over-complex activities, and unrealistic demands on the Afghan bureaucracy (to relocate from Kabul, decentralize decisionmaking, and undertake dramatic new initiatives in underdeveloped rural districts).

The first two objections can be met without much difficulty. DAI addressed the first in a meeting with NE/TECH, arguing that the field study offered more knowledge and insight on rural development problems than had previously been assembled for any district in Afghanistan. The fundamental question in reviewing the project design, therefore, was deciding when enough information had been collected. The Mission's views on this subject were stated in a cable: "The purpose of the...experiment is to provide answers. If answers are already available, there is no need to experiment."[23]

DAI did not become involved in debate over the second issue until after the fact. In early April 1977, a specialist from NE/TECH arrived in Afghanistan with the assignment to resolve outstanding questions affecting the project. Because the project had been billed as "experimental," this specialist insisted that it should have been designed along formal scientific lines. He complained that adequate measures had not been taken to control for external variation, and that insufficient attention had been given to the selection of a "representative" area in Afghanistan for the project. The latter point, he emphasized, was essential if the results of the project were to be replicated in other districts. If anything was to be learned for such replication, it would also be necessary to select a second district for control purposes, so that the course of rural development in the two districts could be rigorously compared.

At a technical level, there was no justification for presuming the existence of a "representative" district. The specialist misjudged the potential of the project's information system, through which it would be possible to compare adaptive and non-adaptive behavior within the district itself. Meaningful "controls" could be established to permit the interpretation of field tests in small group settings, which was the appropriate level for activities to begin.

These difficulties may have stemmed from too literal a reading, on the part of the specialist and others in AID/Washington, of the characterization of the project as an "experiment" and too general an explanation of the adaptive field-testing methodology in the DAI study. An extended discussion of this issue, and some guidelines on the operational meaning of "experimentation," are presented in Chapter 7. In any event, these demands caused considerable confusion in the USAID Mission and produced an indecisive response, which further slowed the project's progress through the review/approval system.

The third issue, concerning appropriate design components, is one upon which professionals are likely to disagree. If one client within AID had firmly decided that the project was too ambitious, DAI could have provided a scaled-down version utilizing a more gradual, lower-profile approach. One possible source of this objection was NE/TECH's uncertainty that the Mission's desire for a large and visible country program was appropriate. Yet the thrust of the project as designed was limited to one district, with planning assistance at the provincial and national levels, to include four technical assistance personnel, not a large percentage increase for the overall USAID complement in Kabul.

The Mission felt that NE/TECH intended to force the retraction of the project as designed. If so, it was successful. NE/TECH insists that its questions, requests for more information, and insistence upon methodological changes were part of a necessary review role to ensure that AID's money would benefit the rural target population. Thus the Mission was characterized as overreacting, since the first PP amendment was never actually rejected or disapproved. The end result was, however, a "rejected" project, since the final revised PP (approved on August 26, 1977) virtually elminated the IRD component. This part of the project was reduced to the provision of one planning advisor to: (1) help develop an area-specific rural development strategy, and (2) give the Mission access to the organizational survey of rural development activities in Afghanistan. Forward action in the field had not begun thirteen months after the original design team departed Kabul.

One real problem in determining the reasons for the difference in perceptions is the undefined nature of the AID/Washington approval process. In the past projects have often been delayed by endless requests by AID/Washington for "more data" before proceeding to the next phase (which may be redesign) and major changes in project thrust.[24] This may sometimes reflect uncertainties within the line of command, in which case diversionary tactics rather than direct attack ensure the best chance of winning bureaucratic battles. In the case of Afghanistan, even if it was not the intent of NE/TECH to kill the project, the signals sent to the Mission gave that distinct impresseion and were so interpreted. The fact that the Afghanistan case did happen suggests that devising a review/approval process using better defined command/decision functions would help Missions to interpret technical responses to project submissions.

Rationalization of the Washington review and approval process is needed. Is Afghanistan an instance of AID/Washington intervening to stop a "bad" project, either by rejecting or fundamentally revising it? Or is this a case of a Washington bureau merely attempting to ensure that its assumptions and priorities are included in the specifics of project design? What should be the responsibility of the Technical Support Office? Does it speak for AID/Washington (as the frustrated Mission staff apparently believed)? What might have happened if:

- NE/TECH had continuity of staff assigned to the project, to prevent inconsistencies in policy and communications to the field?

- The Mission had senior leadership willing and able to take the case above the technical level, and professional staff able to meet the challenge of the NE/TECH specialist? and

- All parties, including DAI, had been assembled in a room to iron out methodologies and design differences?

Since these questions are hypothetical, only speculative answers are possible. The odds are strong, however, that the Afghanistan project would have been salvaged; although salvaging would have been time consuming and, in the absence of a clearly defined decision process, would still have meant securing agreement across a wide spectrum of groups about what exactly should be done. Instead, it consumed $50,000 of AID's money studying a district whose selection was first approved by AID/Washington and then changed for the wrong reasons. It overmatched an experienced rural development staff in NE/TECH with an underequipped Mission to the point that the Mission could not sustain a dialogue or participate in the debate. Most important, it stopped any forward progress in bringing AID-supported development to rural Afghanistan. Chapter 9 reflects upon the possibility of restructuring the AID review/approval system so that the experience will not be repeated in future projects.

OTHER OBJECTIONS

A series of miscellaneous concerns are reflected in the approval of several projects, which are either unique to the project design or represent unanticipated political problems. The Upper Volta Oncho Project is an example of the former. This project involved the resettlement of villages that had been freed of onchocerciasis (river blindness). At the time that the PRP was written, the design team investigated the health hazards of resettlement and was assured that, although spraying for fly eradication had not taken place in the proposed area, it would begin at the time of the scheduled resettlement.

The project was designed after verifying that the oncho elimination program was on schedule. The question of determining when an area would be considered ready for resettlement was not raised until the fourth PP review, eight months after the Project Paper was submitted. At this time, the Mission was asked to supply a status report on the WHO Oncho Control Program. Criteria had been developed by the Oncho Control Program for evaluating when an area was free of onchocerciasis, based on entomological data (fly counts), rather than epidemiological data (disease transmission), since the latter would take several years to verify. The Mission recommended that the project be approved immediately and that the Oncho Control Program certify that an area was free before project funds would be committed for resettlement. The Mission also determined that most of the area would have met the established criteria by the time the project began (August 1977). This satisfied AID/Washington.[25]

This problem was only resolved when AID/Washington agreed to use the quantitative measure of health safety established by the WHO Oncho Control Program as a basis for initiating project activities. It should be pointed out that this potential health hazard is extremely difficult to evaluate and that the entomological criterion, while second-best, has satisfied other donor agencies that have resumed resettlement assistance in the area. The curious aspect of this case is how something so fundamental to project success was seemingly overlooked during the design as well as much of the review process.

There are three projects that experienced delays in the approval process due to unanticipated political problems: the human rights issues raised by the new Administration, and a policy review of relations with one country.

One of these, the Chile Farm Management Project, has been delayed indefinitely; all Agency assistance to the country has been suspended until the human rights questions can be resolved. The project was approved, however, during the Development Assistance Executive Committee (DAEC) review a month after it was submitted. At this writing there is no indication of when Agency assistance might resume in Chile.

The other case affected by human rights considerations was the Ethiopia Rehabilitation Project. Here the delays were temporary. The mini-PP was submitted in April 1977. In May, representatives of the State Department and the Policy Bureau in the Agency concluded that Ethiopia had violated the human rights of its citizens. This decision was manifested in meetings of the World Bank, where the United States voted negatively on a loan recommended for Ethiopia. When it came up again shortly thereafter, the United States abstained during the vote.

This was ultimately resolved by concluding that Ethiopia had not violated the minimum standards for human rights. The issue was complex. People had been jailed or killed without benefit of trial; yet the revolution had increased the real freedom of many of the poorer people. A rapid resolution of the problem was further complicated by restrictions placed on the amount of communication between the Mission and AID/Washington. Still, compared to other projects, the delays were minimal. The entire review and resolution of the human rights question in Ethiopia took about one month.

The last political delay to be discussed took place in Ghana. While the District Development Project was being designed, the Government of Ghana revoked an invitation it had extended to Secretary of State Kissinger to visit the country. In response, U.S. Government policy toward Ghana was extensively reviewed, briefly holding up approval of all new programs for that country.

NOTES

[1] In Chapter 9 overall reflections on appropriate review/approval processes are presented, giving consideration to steps already taken by AID to streamline the system. Particular emphasis is placed on what is needed to move projects based on a process approach through approval to implementation.

[2] For a further discussion of the relationship between quality of project design and what happens during the review/approval process, see Chapter 5.

[3] See Annex A for a more detailed discussion of the legislative history.

[4] Foreign Assistance Act of 1961, Amended Part III, Chapter I, General Provision.

[5] Memo from GC/AFR on "Entente Livestock II," February 20, 1976.

[6] Ethiopia, Ghana, Niger, Tanzania - VD, and both Upper Volta projects.

[7] The Tanzania - VD project was approved in July 1978.

[8] Cables from AID/Washington, 6/12/77 and 6/16/77.

[9] From a review of the unclassified cable traffic during this period, it appears that there were other forms of communication between AID/Washington and the Mission. Probably AID/Washington was providing the Mission with reasons for the delay in project approval and with details of what the Mission Director would have to do with the new authority delegated to him in order to comply with the statutes of the Foreign Assistance Act. Later cable traffic suggested that AID/Washington did not challenge the Mission Director's authority to approve the project, but did attempt to provide him with guidance on what Mission Directors should do to comply with statutory regulations. Such specific instructions were not included in the new directives sent to the Mission Directors.

[10] Section 611(a)(1) does not specify who within the Agency is responsible for compliance. Moreover, it relates to the obli-

gation of funds and not to the authorization of funds. It is possible therefore, to get a project approved and authorized and then delegate to the Mission the authority to determine compliance with Section 611(a)(1).

[11] Cable USAID/Ouagadougou to AID/Washington, 10/30/76.

[12] "Obligation" is the language of the Foreign Assistance Act. Since this is the act that requires adequate prior planning, it is the "obligation" of AID monies that is considered under the heading of 611(a)(1).

[13] This increase is not reflected in the tables and calculations in this document, since the total was reached after June 1978.

[14] The anguish such interminable delays cause a field mission attempting to assist a cooperating country is illustrated by the Tanzania example. Upon receiving the cable from Washington calling for new 611(a)(1) planning, USAID responded directly to the Deputy Director of the Africa Bureau, Haven North:

> Subj: Completion of ARP/VDP Design - 621-0143
>
> Refs: A. State 011808 B. State 009349
>
> 1. Per Reference B and your offer of help unravel "undue delays" in AID/W support efforts, we have a problem.
>
> 2. In September, USAID Assistant Director and Agricultural Economist participated in PC and EPRC reviews of subject project. During EPRC meeting we agreed to stipulations regarding 611(a) requirements for road and water activities since these caused concern. Mission and REDSO are well on way to completing these components and understood AID/W was to prepare authorizing memo containing conditions agreed at EPRC.
>
> 3. Now we receive Reference A reporting on PC meeting held over one month ago that raises whole new design and procedural issues regarding 611 requirements for agriculture and other economic activities and levying upon Mission further extensive design work. We under impression that first PC meeting last September was for purpose of identifying totality of issues for final resolution at subsequent EPRC referenced paragrah 2 above. None of these new issues were raised in any way during PC or EPRC meetings. Also, in view February approval date given to Prime Minister during your December visit, we very surprised these new tasks have been imposed. Following your visit, both Prime Minister and regional officials anticipated technician arrival by July. In

fact, Tanzania Government has already obtained housing and office space. If AID/W insists on pursuing this very difficult course of action and unexpected, spontaneously growing list of design requirements, we foresee project obligation may not occur at any time in FY 1978. By their very nature, agricultural production and other economic activities will vary greatly in view myriad village agriculture and alternative income-generating enterprises now underway in the three districts.

4. 611(a) planning for agricultural production and other economic activities can only be done in any reasonable way during Phase I of project during which time data to be gathered and project activities identified for district programs. Besides involving several additional person-months of work, we believe that attempting to provide this information prior to completing of District plans prejudices outcome of Phase I and destroys Mission intent to base project upon local initiatives. AID/W must decide whether it supports genuine village decision making (Title IX) or AID planning and control. The former follows the Congressional mandate, Tanzania Government decentralization and original project design. The latter represents AID traditional and out of date way of doing business. The two approaches are incompatible.

5. Very concerned that 611 and other legal requirements will continue to tie up Bureau with effect that it impossible to get project approved in less than one year from time of PP submission, as was recently the case with USAID/T seed and research PP revisions. There simply must be better way to get projects moving. Since Bureau on record that this project first priority among FY 78 new starts, we know you share our interest and that of Tanzania Government to proceed as rapidly as possible.

6. Action requested: As minimum, request you press to secure late March authorization total project with Mission Director given authority to approve 611 for agriculture and other activities. Allotment of dollars 1.9 million to follow so that Phase I planning and procurement road and water equipment can proceed. Using work already done on roads and Remington data on 611 water component and with Depp assistance, Mission will rewrite relevant portions of PP for Depp to handcarry end of February. Once Phase I completed, Mission Director can make determination regarding satisfaction 611(a) requirements prior to obligation FY 79 funds for implementation agricultural and other remaining activities.

7. Following your answer this appeal, Mission will report back to Prime Minister and regional officials regarding likely commencement project activities so that Tanzania Government expectations do not continue to exceed our ability to respond. Walker (Dar es Salaam 272, 23 January 1978).

The technical assistance team may be in place (if all goes well) in April 1979, twenty months after completion of the first Project Paper.

[15] A directive in the Africa Bureau now requires that the Executive Project Review Committee be chaired by the Division Director, presumably to invest it with more authority.

[16] For purposes of consistency, Country Development Officers and Regional Development Officers in Sahelian countries are referred to as Mission Directors.

[17] See *Project Development in East and Southern Africa,* op. cit., p. 74.

[18] Part 216, "Environmental Procedures," Rules and Regulations of the Agency for International Development, *Federal Register,* June 30, 1976.

[19] Cable USAID/Addis Ababa to AID/Washington, 7/5/77.

[20] Regarding Tanzania Farmer Training Project:

Dar es Salaam cable 0833, March 9, 1976

Ref: (a) State 54770, (b) DAR 0813

1. Mission staff believes issues and misunderstandings that have arisen from Project Papers can be boiled down to the skills desired of the technicians stationed in the MATIs.

2....Believe Mission and Tanzania Government have mutual understanding of these skills. Below is the job criteria as rewritten by the Ministry of Agriculture:

'As pointed out earlier, the critical USAID input will be the four technical experts assigned to the partcipating MATIs. These experts will be a part of the regular staff assigned to the farmer training wings. At each participating MATI, the technical expert will:

Help design the research effort necessary for building an understanding of farmer behavior;
Assist the various Tanzanian institutions in testing various training and extension methods, and the different technological packages;
Train the MATI staff and students in data collection and analysis techniques as well as provide inputs into regional and district planning; and
Assist as part of the MATI team in dispensing technical assistance of an appropriate nature to the villages concerned.

'The technical expert should have a basic agricultural background and experience in two-way communications, data-gathering techniques, and the analysis of research data. To maximize their effectiveness, they will have to be well integrated into the MATI staff.

'Major criteria for the selection of these technical experts include:

Four to six years experience as an agricultural or rural development specialist. The individuals selected must have an understanding of traditional farming systems and experience in introducing changes into these systems.

The individual must also have experience in the design and conduct of farmer and extension worker training programs.

Background in applied research methodology, to include experience in the design of data collection instruments and in the analysis of the data collected. The individual must be able to assess the capabilities of the MATIs and other Tanzanian institutions for doing this type of work, and to develop a program within these capabilities.

Academic background should include a minimum of M.S. degree with a preference given for Ph.D. The individual should have one degree in agriculture with supporting studies in economic development, sociology, applied anthropology or communications.

Language capabilities in Swahili. This will facilitate communication with staff and farmers and allow closer monitoring of training and research program. Provision for language training for staff members and their spouses is included in the project, though if possible, Swahili speakers should be recruited.

Willingness to live and work under Tanzania MATI conditions.

3. While this includes both social science and production aspects in original proposal the emphasis has been shifted from data gathering to agriculture production though we emphasize both parts are to be fully implemented in the project.

4. Reason for Ministry of Agriculture position known to [Mission] Director....

5. In order to assure social science/data collection activities receive desired emphasis, Ministry of Agriculture has agreed to a fifth project position to be stationed in Dar. The skills of this individual position would be along the lines of the bio-data sheet presented to Ministry of Agriculture. Essentially this means social science/rural development capabilities with agriculture production not essential. He would oversee and work with the MATIs and U.S. technicians on the data gathering team....

6. We believe this to be a workable solution if right people are recruited and urge acceptance.

[Cable abbreviations have been spelled out for clarification.]

Regarding Tanzania Village Development Project,

Dar es Salaam cable 3733, September 13, 1977

Ref: State 216795

....

9. Concerning paragraph F of the referenced telegram we agree balance in manpower may need adjustment and concur agriculture skills of prime importance. Can discuss.

[Cable abbreviations have been spelled out for clarification.]

[21] Memo from General Counsel to AFR/DR 1/7/77. The Farmer Training Project was subsumed into the Agricultural Manpower Development Project, which was being implemented by this consortium.

[22] One group in the Agency advocated hiring agricultural specialists. In contrast the PP recommended hiring individuals with training in the dynamics of rural development, of which agricultural training is but one aspect. This issue will only be resolved when the technical assistance team is actually selected from among the competitive bidders. (Proposals were submitted January 24, 1979.)

[23] Cable USAID/Kabul to AID/Washington, 5/7/77. This is certainly not to argue that the design was flawless or that the output of the study perfectly suited the needs of the Project Paper.

[24] The reader is again referred to *Project Development in East and Southern Africa,* op. cit., p. 73, for a discussion of the use of the techniques in the Africa Bureau. The reader is also referred to the literature on bureaucratic dynamics for a discussion of this tactic (E. Bardach, op. cit.).

[25] This process involved a series of meetings of AID/Washington, USAID, WHO, and Government of Upper Volta representatives, and consumed five additional months.

4
Organization and Implementation

INTRODUCTION

Although design work for several projects was performed in 1975 and early 1976, only three of the twelve projects under review have an implementation history to allow insights to be drawn. One is the Colombia Small Farmer Development Project, for which the loan agreement was signed in June 1976 and implementation activities started by the host country in January 1977.[1] The second is the Zaire North Shaba Project, for which approval was obtained in September 1976 and implementation begun (in the sense that a technical assistance contract with DAI was signed) in July 1977. The third is the Ethiopia Rehabilitation Project (Gamo Gofa) with pre-implementation technical assistance initiated in mid-September 1977.

This chapter has two major sections. In the first section, the organizational arrangements for the implementation of the twelve projects are described briefly, with specific reference to the main options for structuring projects in developing countries. Because of the complexity of this issue, as well as the necessary reference to the literature and projects outside the sample, the discussion of the problems of organizational arrangements is in Chapter 8.

In the second section, implementation problems are considered from the vantage point of the beginnings of implementation in the three projects underway. Here the problems of making the projects workable are examined with a view to improving project design. Even with only three cases, many difficulties appeared, suggesting the need for implementing analysis as a critical study area in development assistance projects.

ORGANIZATIONAL ARRANGEMENTS FOR IMPLEMENTATION

Appropriate arrangements for project organization must be based on the project context. Identical formal arrangements can function quite differently in dissimilar environments or with dissimilar people. Nevertheless, by looking at the basic management structure and operating responsibilities of the twelve projects, it should be possible to identify certain basic patterns.

In dealing with governments and development organizations in Third World countries, project organization options are limited. The organizational strategies used in the twelve projects under review can be classified as follows:

- Working through traditional line ministries (usually the Ministry of Agriculture) at the national level, with ministry staff located at subnational levels to carry out project activities;
- Working through subnational governments or government agencies, whose staff serve to carry out project activities;
- Working through integrated development agencies at the national level, with subnational arms that coordinate and/or carry out project activities; or
- Working through special project management organizations created for the unique purpose of implementing the project.

Table 4.1 shows how the twelve projects under review fit into these four categories.

The Ethiopia Rehabilitation Project offers one example of implementation arrangements that appeared straightforward during the design phase. The activities were to be carried out by a subnational government -- the province -- although coordinated with the work of the national Relief and Rehabilitation Commission (RCC). Four months into the pre-implementation phase, the organizational arrangements have evolved into something far more complex.

The pre-implementation project was to provide development assistance to one part of a province, approximately fifty percent of the total area, through the establishment of a Provincial Development Office

TABLE 4.1

ORGANIZATIONAL ARRANGEMENTS FOR PROJECT IMPLEMENTATION: FOUR BASIC MANAGEMENT STRUCTURES

Project	(1) National-Level Ministries	(2) Subnational Agencies	(3) Integrated National-Level Agencies	(4) Project Management Units
Afghanistan			X	
Chile	X			
Colombia	X			
Ethiopia		X		
Ghana		X		
Haiti	X			
Niger[a]			X	
Tanzania - FT	X			
Tanzania - VD		X		
Upper Volta - OP			X	
Upper Volta - WP		X		
Zaire				X

Column: (1) Traditional national-level line ministries operating through staff at subnational levels.

(2) Subnational governments or government agencies operating through local staff.

(3) Integrated national-level development agencies that coordinate and/or carry out project activities through their own staff at subnational levels.

(4) Specially created project management organizations.

[a] The Niger project was designed with a focus on decentralization, but redesigned and approved with more power concentrated in the national-level agency.

(PDO). The PDO acts on behalf of the entire province, while USAID/Addis supports operations in one portion of the province. This particular area was chosen to coincide with the operations of the line agency, the RRC, which had originally signed the Project Agreement. There is and remains an unclear relationship between the PDO and the local activities of the RRC, and the latter is not in complete harmony with the Revolutionary Campaign and Development Committee, which has overall policy responsibility for Government activities in the province. The PRP design team had correctly gauged that, to be successful, the project must operate under the overall umbrella and jurisdiction of the Provincial Committee.[2] This has been the actual organization during pre-implementation, with the PDO and the Rural Development Specialist established as an official arm of this Provincial Committee.

The project requires close cooperation with the RRC Office, since the latter has gasoline, the funding release authority for the USAID/Addis grant (for administrative costs), and contact with and knowledge of the outlying ethnic groups (peasant associations) in remote Southern Gamo Gofa. The project, if it operates as it should, hopes to use the PDO to coordinate all development activities in a way that will return the policy committee and the RRC to a cooperative working relationship. It is not a straightforward or easy set of initial working relationships.

The USAID grant can be interpreted as restricted to portions of two of the four districts within the Province of Gamo Gofa, which presents interesting possibilities for conflict and confusion. The Provincial Policy Committee, seizing upon the concept of integrated , mutually supporting development activities, has assigned its only non-specific office to the PDO -- the motor pool, including vehicle maintenance. This gives the PDO transportation for work in the grant area; it also tasks the PDO with providing transportation and maintenance for areas of the province outside those included in the grant. This action by the policy committee is not duplicity: the line agencies are charged for transport and maintenance services, including a surplus over cost (certainly not a "profit" in socialist Ethiopia), which is to be added to the budget of the PDO. A wiser solution, seen from the vantage point of four months into the pre-implementation, would be for the grant to specifically rather than *de facto* support the overall PDO, with subproject funds limited to Southern

Gamo Gofa. These details and complexities were not foreseen in the project design.

In the Colombia Small Farmer Development Project, personnel shifts at the policy level, after the project design had been completed, have resulted in a decision by ICA to implement this project through its existing (traditional) line divisions, with the thought that, if the new methods are successful, they would be more easily integrated into other ongoing operations. The original plan, which was to have special units undertake implementation and evaluation, has been rejected by senior management. The resulting diffusion of decisionmaking responsibility throughout ICA has further weakened the experimental nature of the project. Because it amounts to one more task added to the duties of field supervisors, this project will tend to resemble closely ongoing activities undertaken by this research and extension institute.

One of the major lessons, by the implementers, is the tremendous importance of arriving at optimal organizational arrangements for project implementation. The arrangements must fit into the administrative structure of the host country in order to promote effective implementation of the project as designed. The *Strategies* report made little mention of this issue, but subsequent work has made it apparent that the question of "how to do it" is also a question of "how to organize to do it." The answer is not always readily apparent. Chapter 8 discusses the question of organizational arrangements for implementation in greater detail, considering the selection of a management structure appropriate to the project's environment and assignment.

THE NEED FOR IMPLEMENTATION ANALYSIS IN AID'S PROJECT DESIGN

Implementation analysis, in the context of development assistance, should be the comparative study of implementation problems, their causes, and solutions for individual projects. This calls for a careful matching of the needs of the project -- resources, commodities, technical assistance, transportation, budget flexibility -- and the delivery capacity of both the development assistance donor and the host country implementing agencies. There is a knowledge void on this subject: the sadder-but-wiser lessons have not been documented across projects and incorporated into the development literature.[3]

The organizational issues discussed in the previous section can create serious problems in project implementation. In Colombia, Zaire and Ethiopia, the following additional problem categories surfaced as being important:

- Selecting appropriate technical assistance;
- Overly optimistic implementation plans;
- Inadequate implementation incentives within AID;
- The release and use of project and contract funds;
- Problems of continuity (AID, host country and technical assistance staff); and
- The need for AID's leverage in realizing project objectives.

Selecting Appropriate Technical Assistance

In the three projects under implementation -- Colombia, Zaire and Ethiopia -- there are striking contrasts in the need for (actual and perceived) and the arrangements to provide appropriate technical assistance.

The host country implementing agency in Colombia, ICA, is staffed with numerous Ph.D.-holding specialists and even more master's degree holders, many educated in the U.S. but an increasing number from ICA's own graduate school. Given this predominance of locally available talent, including staff with direct experience in small farmer development programs, two distinct categories of technical assistance were proposed:

- Assistance in the development of information systems necessary to generate conclusions from the testing of various project components. ICA's experience in evaluation was fairly routine, limited to post-project reviews. The project designers believed that this project would need a far more innovative system of ongoing review, and scheduled up to thirty person-months of social science specialists into the project.

- Short-term technical expertise in various aspects of agronomy, water utilization, appropriate technology, and other related fields where constraints to increasing small farmer productivity and income might arise.

In the final stages of negotiation prior to the submission of the Project Paper, the AID project officer changed the technical assistance funding from a grant to a loan, thus reducing the amount of Colombian local currency support needed for the project. AID traditionally limits the amount of grant-funded technical assistance for the more developed countries, but there had been no previous concern regarding the grant portion of the Colombia project.[4] The host country implementing agency has not drawn upon any of the technical assistance funds, and has not had the internal capacity or the incentives to implement the project as designed, particularly the information and monitoring aspects so critical to the adaptive field-testing of various project components.

In Zaire the technical assistance was grant-funded under a contract paid by AID in dollars. The specifications called for a team of nine, later increased to ten professionals, permanently stationed in Zaire, and an additional forty person-months of short-term assistance and home office support. The Project Agreement was signed on September 30, 1976, and the request for proposals was issued on February 25, 1977. The search for a contracting organization was as thorough and competitive as any in AID's recent history. The review of the proposed technical assistance team included:

- Individual interviews with the proposed team members by a seven-person review staff, including a representative of the Government of Zaire. Three separate interviews with each person were taped for the use of reviewers who were not present at the time.

- Team interviews, which were videotaped in a formal project approach and problem solving setting.

- Three successive calls for revisions in the submissions, including personnel, timing, work plans, approach, and methodology.

As a result of the interviews, the GOZ representative decided that one specialist proposed for long-term assignment was unacceptable. Prior to the project team's departure, an additional long-term specialist dropped out, leaving two vacancies. DAI, which received the contract to provide the technical assistance after the extensive selection process, was able to fill the second position with an acceptable candidate. That specialist was in place in Zaire along with the rest of the initial team three months after the contract for technical assistance was signed. The problems of filling the first position have been illustrative once again of the problem of who makes decisions. A candidate was nominated for this position in September and subsequently rejected, and in January 1978 a new candidate was submitted for consideration.

For the Ethiopia Rehabilitation Project, USAID and the PRP design team decided upon an evolutionary approach to project development, using a pre-implementation period to build a data base and to test technologies and development approaches. Because of the Ethiopian Government's sensitivities about American technical assistance, the design team limited technical assistance in the pre-implementation period to a Rural Development Specialist, who would act as an advisor to the provincial administration, with the support of a series of short-term technical experts over an eight-month period.

USAID turned to DAI to provide this technical assistance, because of its role in the design of the project, and the relative ease of contracting for short-term assistance. A three-month search was conducted to find a Rural Development Specialist with strong planning and management experience, as well as the social and political sensitivity to work in a situation where a previous American technician had just been expelled by the Ethiopian Government. Such an individual was found and assigned to Gamo Gofa for a test period of three months during which DAI, USAID and the Government of Ethiopia could judge his effectiveness. USAID then wrote a Mission contract to cover the remaining four months of the pre-implementation period.

DAI was also to provide the necessary supporting technical experts. However, the government has rejected this assistance, contending that they should do the work themselves. During the project design, the technical assistance requirements had been discussed and had received the approval of the participating government agencies. However, a massive turnover in personnel during the year following the PRP design exercise left only one official with any knowledge about the project. This, combined with increased sensitivities toward foreigners, has created a situation where the project is not receiving adequate technical assistance.

It is too early to predict the outcomes of these three projects, for the only test of the appropriateness of technical assistance (and other design elements) is the actual developmental changes that result. Nevertheless, these examples do show various mechanisms and possible problems in the structuring of the technical assistance component of a project.

Overly Optimistic Implementation Plans

Ethiopia

On September 15, 1977 approximately one year after the PRP design team completed its fieldwork in Gamo Gofa Province, Ethiopia, DAI assigned a Rural Development Specialist to assist in the eight-month pre-implementation phase of the Southern Gamo Gofa Rehabilitation Project.[5] He had been preceded in Addis Ababa by DAI's PRP design team leader, who left behind week-by-week recommendations on how the specialist might begin his work. In retrospect, this list makes fascinating reading, since the project, after three and one-half months, is approximately through week four of the recommended timetable. This noncongruence between what might have happened if all worked well, and what did in fact happen, provides valuable insights into the beginning of project implementation.

To begin with no one in the Province was aware that the advisor was arriving; no advance warning had been given, nor preparations made. In spite of the best introductory efforts of the USAID Deputy Director, who made a special trip to get the project underway, this was an inauspicious beginning. The Project Agreement had been signed at the national level by the head of the Relief and Rehabilitation Commission (RRC) and countersigned by the Province Administrator, who could not behave as though development funds would appear until, in fact, the check was in the bank.[6] In spite of strenuous and time-consuming efforts of the PRP team to involve officials at provincial, district and local levels -- including having them participate in the field collection efforts -- a year later there remaind only one official, the head of the local chapter of the RRC, who had knowledge of the project and remembered the PRP design efforts. DAI's Rural Development Specialist, assigned to the still nonexistent Provincial Development Office, wrote of his initial week in the Provincial Capital of Arba Minch:

> It became immediately apparent that the local representative of the Ministry of Agriculture, concurrently Chairman of the Rural Development Sub-committee of the Provincial Revolutionary Administration and Development Committee, and Chief of the Provincial Development Office had NEVER HEARD OF THIS PROJECT AND HAD NO PRIOR UNDERSTANDING OF IT WHATSOEVER. He had never seen <u>any</u> of the project documents and had never met any of the USAID personnel that had previously visited Gamo Gofa, nor had been briefed by anyone in the RRC or in the Administrator's office.[7]

In the following weeks this problem was overcome, but it set back the implementation of the project.

Zaire

DAI contracted to provide technical assistance to this project in July 1977 and dispatched the first technical field staff to the regional center in eastern Zaire in the first week of the contract. By the end of August seven permanent staff were in place and two others were being sought.[8] The DAI home office, which helped design the project, and the permanent technical assistance team, knew that it would be an extremely difficult assignment. Six months later the enormities of the undertaking are becoming increasingly clear, as is the possibility that little progress may be possible within the environment given the implementation arrangements that have evolved so far in the project. Almost a counterpart to the Ethiopia assignment, this project has undergone an uphill struggle as a result of initial implementation activities that have proven to be inadequate for mobilization of project resources in the difficult environment of Zaire. With the benefit of hindsight one can see that more attention to the details of mobilization constraints would have avoided many of the problems.

Those familiar with Zaire, and in particular with Shaba Province in the east, have always questioned whether a development program was possible there.

The area is remote, isolated, and caught up in the political turmoil that has rocked South Shaba for decades. In a country afflicted with rampant inflation, chronic shortages of foreign exchange, and pervasive corruption, increasing the quality of life of the minority ethnic groups in the East was never considered an easy task. One member of the DAI design team flatly stated that the odds were against any positive outcomes from development assistance. Optimism, however, prevailed.

After the Project Paper fieldwork was completed, the area suffered three setbacks:

- The weekly air service to Kongolo, the project's headquarters, was discontinued, leaving the area 60 hours by train away from the regional center (Lubumbashi);

- The military moved into the area in large numbers, permeating what had been primarily a civilian society with the inevitable and occasionally realized potential for coercion and conflict; and

- The ramifications of the war in South Shaba have virtually eliminated supplies of gas and oil, and merely getting in the queue -- the priority list -- has proved to be a major challenge for the field team and USAID. Few vehicles move and electricity and water supplies are nonexistent. There was little the team could do in the field. Until November they lived in Lubumbashi, when those staff without family relocated to Kongolo.

Fifteen months after the signing of the Project Agreement, the project is staggering toward effective implementation. For the realities of North Shaba, this is an appropriate schedule. For the quick-paced requirements of AID's implementation scheduling, it is cause for concern and explanation. Both USAID and DAI felt that the full ten-person team could be fielded at project commencement, but experience with the difficult pre-implementation activities has shown that a small mobilization team could have produced a more efficient and less conflict-laden start-up. This would have necessitated a change in the deployment schedule for the Zairois staff and might have dampened local enthusiasm for the project. The difficulties of trying to predict how quickly a Third World government or the AID bureaucracy can or will act make any given implementation schedule uncertain.

Inadequate Implementation Incentives with AID

Colombia and Ethiopia

Between the signing of the Project Agreement and the beginning of implementation, the USAID office and AID support offices in Washington often have tasks that must be performed if the implementation schedule is to be met. In Colombia, where no AID commodities were furnished, funding was released to the implementing agency. This constitutes minimal tasking of the Mission and in this instance worked without difficulty.

In Ethiopia the vehicle that was ordered arrived on schedule, providing transportation for the Rural Development Specialist assigned to the Province, who was himself made available under a rapid-response contract. Since this project is in a pre-implementation phase, there was no need to supply housing, appliances or other AID logistical support.

Zaire

In Zaire it became necessary for the Mission to put forth large expenditures of time and effort if the implementation plan were to be met.

The Project Agreement was signed on September 30, 1976. It stipulated a schedule for dispatching the Zairois and U.S. field teams, as well as a set of Conditions Precedent for the GOZ to meet, including the nomination of team members and the establishment of a fund to support the project. The GOZ acted faster and with greater commitment to the project than was anticipated, establishing a support fund that was nearly double the stipulated amount. By April 1977 Zairois field team members were moving to the project area as scheduled, but the AID bureaucracy at that time was just receiving proposals for the technical assistance contract that would provide support for the project.

During the project design it was clear that considerable improvement to existing buildings would be required before American families or Zairois senior staff could move into the area safely and with minimal amenities. The implementation schedule called for housing rehabilitation to be completed on April 1, in time for the arrival of the project teams. However, USAID/Kinshasa did not start the work until June 1977, having in the interim opted to investigate an alternative that proved to be overly expensive. Adequate housing was not available for the U.S. team until after they were in-country more than six months. The Zairois field staff simply made do with whatever housing arrangements were available.

Although they were ordered after the signing of the project agreement, no AID vehicles were been made available to the project until late 1978. The GOZ purchased six pickups from their own funds. USAID placed an additional $25,000 in DAI's contract to provide for the rapid purchase and shipment of motorcycles, but even these were not available to the field staff until December 1977.

To summarize, the Government of Zaire was well ahead of USAID in the provision of staff, support and commodities to this project. Unfortunately, the system within AID produced slippages in generating the PIO/T, in securing competitive bids for the technical assistance, in the rehabilitation or construction of housing, in the purchase of applicances, in the arrival of office supplies and furniture and radios to facilitate contact with the isolated team in the field, and in the release of loan and counterpart funds.[9]

With time the deficiencies are being, or have been, corrected. The lack of support when and as needed prevented the project from meeting the implementation schedule. This discrepancy between Project Agreement and the arrival of project support has strong ramifications for other AID "New Directions" projects designed to reach remote and isolated areas.

If the USAID office overseas is viewed as a system, there is an interesting interpretation to the lack of field support in Zaire. When the decision-making took place at the level of the Mission Director, and when he was available after returning from home leave, actions were taken. There has been no lack of support or enthusiasm from Mission leadership. However the vast majority of implementation activities are considered routine (ordering the vehicles, repairing the houses, buying appliances, establishing the loan fund, writing the PIO/T), and these routine actions are not given high priority within the AID system. Instead they are assigned to those whose careers depend more on adherence to regulations than on facilitating a difficult rural development project. Such a system tends to produce decisions and action only when a crisis raises the issues well above their normal level. There are few incentives for reacting quickly, overcoming procedural problems, or solving problems in innovative, non-routine ways. In spite of good intentions, positive leadership when called upon, rapid assignment of the technical assistance team, and strong commitment from the Government of Zaire, the project will soon be a year behind schedule. Much of the delay can be attributed to a lack of priority within AID for specific project implementation support activities.

The Release and Use of Project and Contract Funds

The obligation of funds for a project that requires contracted technical assistance can be divided between a contract budget and a project budget. The former is the responsibility of the technical assistance team, and the latter is managed jointly between the technical assistance team and the host country Project Manager, subject to review and approval by USAID. One reasonable method of meeting the costs of technical assistance is to place in the project budget all expenses that must be paid in local currency, including housing, in-country transportation, and the numerous small expenses incurred in the project area.

This was not possible in Zaire, due to the Zairois Project Manager's determination that grant funds from AID, once passed to the Government of Zaire, were to be disbursed according to the regulations of the Government of Zaire -- a very different set of payments, benefits and allowances from those authorized under AID regulations. For this reason all expenses to support the contract team in North Shaba were placed in the dollar contract.[10]

There is a second reason for using the dollar contract: It allows rapid response for critical services or commodities that could be purchased from project funds, but would incur long delays, negating their usefulness. In the Zaire project, due to the absence of USAID-ordered transportation, funds were added to the dollar contract to buy motorcycles for the project. Because of an impending shipping strike, DAI was exempted from formal competitive bidding to fill the order, and the cost-comparison investigation took about ten days. When the Mission's request for this addition to the contract was finally approved by AID/Washington, the purchase and delivery to the loading docks of the motorcycles took two days. Similarly, items in the dollar contract made other necessary purchases possible.[11] If used correctly the dollar contract with the technical assistance team can provide the flexibility lacking in project funds managed by USAID (commodity orders) or as expended by the host country in local currency.

Two special problems, which developed in Ethiopia with the pre-implementation project, illustrate the difficulties of working with project funds to support a provincial development project.

Who Pays for What

This pre-implementation project started in the midst of the Government of Ethiopia's budget year. In the Project Agreement, GOE support included three categories: Staff, Recurring Budget, and Local Labor and Materials. None of these are spendable funds, which apparently was not anticipated in the mini-PP or the Project Agreement. An examination of the budget categories shows why:

- Staff. The PRP calls for a chief of the Provincial Development Office (PDO), deputy, and three subordinate officials plus supporting cast, all furnished by the GOE. The Province has no budget for these personnel, and certainly no surplus government officials who can be detailed to this assignment. In reality, staff to be assigned consisted of already overworked (if they are competent) officials at the Provincial level, to be assigned part-time to the PDO -- ten percent from this officer, fifteen percent from that officer -- to reach the numbers stated in the Project Agreement. This is a common PP sleight-of-hand to generate host country contributions.

  It became clear very early on that, without a full-time deputy working in the PDO, there would be no counterpart for the Rural Development Specialist and no head for the organization. The Province, the line agency (RRC), and USAID agreed to hire a staff for the PDO from special funds, which had not been anticipated in the original Project Agreement. In the absence of this flexibility to change the funding categories and provide for a staff outside the existing personnel at the provincial level, the project would not have moved.

- <u>Recurring Budget</u>. This category has proved to be whatever the PDO needs that the line agency or the Province has and will furnish. Gasoline has been a big item, furnished by the RRD, but such an agreement was not set forth in the project documents; it has been negotiated after the fact. Office space has been another, which the Province just happened to have available but could just as easily not have. This was not known when the agreement was signed. But when supplies or facilities do not exist, as for example when the telephone bills must be paid or the water and electricity charges come due, only the USAID grant funds are available. These were expected to come "from the GOE," but there are no funds within the provincial budget for such expenditures, and therefore no alternative but to make such payments from the "other" category in the USAID grant.

- <u>Local Labor and Materials</u>. This is the category used by project designers to get the host country's contribution up to some necessary level, such as twenty-five percent of the total project costs. In "New Directions" mandate projects, such local contributions, to be matched with PDO technical and material assistance, are to be furnished by the participants in support of subprojects. But these are not spendable funds and can be used to support a project activity only after the government has delivered a good idea, and the outside assistance necessary to make it work, into a local community. They are GOE contributions only in the loose sense that the providers are local citizens of the GOE.

In summary, the host country contribution to the project was agreed to consist of part-time staff who have other full-time duties, non-specific recurring expenses in items that the government has in surplus, and non-spendable local labor and materials. The rest is up to USAID, whose flexibility and willingness to support the project has been outstanding. A less interested or capable Mission could have left the project, the Rural Development Specialist, and the contracting organization with precious little to support the project.

The Release of Funds

In the initial turmoil accompanying the arrival and authentication of DAI's Rural Development Specialist, a host of "Conditions Precedent" remained to be met prior to the release of USAID's grant funding. This included such items as the organization of the Provincial Development Office, staffing, visas, office space, and transportation. Even after the original conditions are met, there are time lags between:

- Meeting the Conditions Precedent and the issuance of the USAID check; and
- The conversion of that check into spendable accounts, with authorized signatures at the local Arba Minch bank.

Only the grant funds were considered "spendable" in the pre-implementation period, but by December 16, three months after the arrival of the Rural Development Specialist, not a dollar of the grant had reached the hands of a vendor or PDO staff member. This put a strain on the entire operation, since little can be accomplished without funds.

USAID released its grant check on December 9, but a week later the authorization cable from the line ministry in Addis Ababa, confirming the valid signatures, had not been received in Arba Minch. Yet there have been salaries to be paid (the driver of the USAID-furnished vehicle, for example) expenses of putting the office into shape, and salaries for the PDO staff including translators, secretaries, guards, drivers and cleaners. It is an interesting dilemma since without such an office the Conditions Precedent are not met, and creating the office generated expenses for which there are no funds. In this instance the solution was found in out-of-pocket payments by the Rural Development Specialist, and the flexibility of the local representative of the line ministry (RRC) supporting the project, who accepted a check from the PDO that was uncashable at the time in exchange for the funds to meet the monthly payroll.

If these problems are known and understood, up-front disbursements can normally be written into long-term technical assistance contracts. But the Rural Development Specialist was funded under a short-term temporary arrangement, which paid only salary and per diem. The time lag in receiving funds not only hinders the "gearing up" of the PDO during pre-implementation, but makes the Provincial Policy Committee uneasy as they see the technical assistance (which is rarely the most important part of the project from the point of view of the host country) arrive long before funds start to flow. Project design must deal directly with questions of the source of start-up funds and the date they will be released. If long delays are foreseen, alternatives must be found.

Problems of Continuity (AID, Host Country and Technical Assistance Staff)

USAID/Bogota project designers had departed post before the Project Agreement was signed. In Ethiopia the project officer, who had made three extensive trips through the remote area of Southern Gamo Gofa, was transferred prior to the assignment of the Rural Development Specialist and the beginning of implementation. In Zaire the Project Design Officer continued with the project only through the first six months and was replaced by a member of the Food and Agriculture Office. This is a continual problem in any large bureaucracy: Long before project implementation begins, the creators, who nursed the idea through to approval, have usually departed. Such changes only add to the already difficult problems of implementation.

Within the host country there are often rapid changes of policy leadership and technical specialists. In Colombia such changes reverberated through the operational and organizational arrangements for the Small Farmer Development Project, shifting implementation to divisions that were not part of the original design. In Ethiopia there remained only one of the previous year's provincial authorities who had participated in the project design. In Zaire only time will tell whether continuity of the remaining staff in remote North Shaba can be maintained.

There is a special problem for technical assistance personnel. Present AID procedures discourage continuity from design, through pre-implementation, on to full implementation.[12] The special problem of pre-implementation in Ethiopia is considered here.

Pre-implementation in the Southern Gamo Gofa Area Rehabilitation Project called for a short contract with one advisor to the Provincial Development Office in Arba Minch, providing his salary and per diem expenses. After three and one-half months, when it was clear that the specialist was acceptable to USAID and the Government of Ethiopia, the contract was rewritten to continue an additional four months. Since there is always the possibility that the full project will meet delays in the review and approval process, or be cancelled by AID/Washington or the Government of Ethiopia, it has not been possible to make arrangements for the long-term support of this specialist. This poses two problems:

- Providing adequate housing for the technical assistance personnel and family. The experienced, Ph.D. social scientist is prepared to live in two hotel rooms for eight months, undergoing a lengthy separation from his family that approaches the limit of his patience. Under strict interpretation of the regulations, AID cannot construct permanent housing, since there is as yet no permanent project. Waiting until after the end of the pre-implementation period to begin construction could mean a twelve- to fourteen-month delay from his initial arrival. This can become a major obstacle to obtaining the right technical assistance personnel for a demanding and complicated assignment. No solution to this problem -- different from but analogous to the housing shortfalls in the Zaire North Shaba Project -- yet exists.

- Maintaining continuity in technical assistance from the pre-implementation into the full project. If the Rural Development Specialist works out well during the pre-implementation period, USAID should ensure that he will be available for the full project. But this is contrary to the underlying philosophy of many contracting offices that technical assistance personnel are interchangeable. One way to avoid a competitive award at the end of the pre-implementation period is to establish the "predominant capability" of one organization to do the job. Yet so long as one Rural Development Specialist looks much like another on paper, there are no predominant capabilities, and neither DAI's candidate who will have committed eight months to a hotel room in Arba Minch, nor the Government of Ethiopia, which has started to work with and understand one foreigner, can be assured that he will be called upon to continue. A solution is to accept a testing period, after which the specialist can be accepted in the position and his continued presence requested by the host government. This request should be accepted by AID as reason for continuation of the contract.

The Need for AID Leverage in Realizing Project Objectives

AID's "New Directions" development projects may have objectives that do not exactly coincide with those of a cooperating host government. So long as there is sufficient overlap, there can be differences with both parties still achieving important goals. Such an arrangement, however, calls for the use of leverage by AID in situations where the natural inclination of the implementing agency does not coincide with the stated objectives of the project.

Such leverage is part of the design process, including the Conditions Precedent incorporated in the Project Agreement. Throughout the project the possibility remains that USAID will stop the disbursements. This, however, amounts to a sledgehammer, which is not useful in fine tuning and adjusting a project during the implementation process. Other more subtle levers include the adroit use and support of technical assistance, the ability of USAID to reach above the project management to higher level policymakers in the host government and the carrot of additional AID funds in the future to override poor operational decisions. The use of such leverage in the three projects studied provides an insight in the role of AID in the implementation of development projects.

Declining Influence in Colombia

In Colombia the World Bank and other bilateral donors are in the process of offering substantial development assistance -- far more than AID could provide. A decision to phase out the USAID Mission over the next few years has considerably diminished the potential for additional U.S. government money. There was little collaboration in design of the Small Farmer Development Project, which eliminated any moral and personal commitment to the project that staff members of the implementing agency might have had. In negotiations with the head of ICA, the USAID Project Officer changed technical assistance from grant to loan funded. This reduced the contribution required of the Colombian Government, which was a higher percentage when calculated on the grant than when calculated on the loan. Such a change made the project more "approvable" in Washington, and more palatable to the GOC.

On the other hand, this change eliminated all leverage that might have been possible through technical assistance. In the absence of outside support and suggestions regarding those elements of the project that are not part of ICA's normal operations, new investigations and approaches have not been tried.

Chain of Command Failure in Ethiopia

A second failure of leverage through technical assistance is only now evident in the Ethiopia project. The provincial government has a great deal of difficulty with the concept that more than one foreign advisor should work in the project. They have rejected suggestions for what would be to them "free" services of an experienced Swedish anthropologist and an American agricultural economist, both of whom have worked previously in the project area. If there had been national-level agreement and backing, the advisors would likely have been welcomed and accepted without question as colleagues of the Rural Development Specialist. Asking the Provincial Policy Committee to make the decision to include more foreign assistance was to demand too much risk-taking in this revolutionary society. No one anticipated the denial at the time the project was designed, as the individuals then in policy positions in Arba Minch supported the idea. In retrospect, including this provision in the Project Agreement would have paved the way for further discussions in the provincial capital. It is likely the project would proceed much faster with additional short-term expertise.[13]

USAID's Role in North Shaba

It is in the difficult environment of North Shaba, Zaire, that the need for the use of leverage held by USAID to improve implementation is most obvious. In an attempt to generate a truly collaborative project, the Zairois Project Manager has been given significant authority and input into the project from early stages, joining the review team to select the contracting organization in Washington, D.C. Early in the project, the Mission forcefully reminded the Project Manager that he was to make the decisions, since in similar projects in Zaire the leadership has often been assumed by the technical assistance team. The Minister of Agriculture has enlarged the Project Manager's authority by determining that he will make all non-policy decisions for the project.

If the selection process for Project Manager has been successful, such designation of authority and responsibility would be most appropriate. But in a new project, in a new area, it is not possible to make that determination. Complaints have come from the Ministry of Agriculture, as well as the field staff, about the lack of USAID support. Although the Zairois have been in the project area for months, working without technical assistance, their efforts appear to be contributing little to the project's objectives from AID's perspectives. However, they are doing it by themselves, with their own government's money. Such an arrangement does not engender a strong willingness to share ideas, receive outside suggestions, or make the project into a cooperative effort.

On a visit in December 1977, the DAI home office project coordinator found that the Project Manager had used the authority he had been delegated to set up a structure that did not allow for meetings between the technical assistance staff and Zairois staff, except with his personal knowledge and approval. There were no counterparts for anyone but the DAI team leader, and no latitude for two rural development specialists to make any substantive inputs into project activities. The Project Manager made all decisions and controls all activities. His focus, in consonance with his background, is in agronomic research. The technical assistance team, however useful in providing the logistical and infrastructure support to the project, has yet to make a significant contribution to the planning or implementation of project activities in the field. The question now is whether USAID can use its leverage and access to national policy decisionmakers to resolve the situation.

Perhaps the most forceful lesson learned from the Zaire experience is that USAID Missions must exercise strong leadership in the implementation of development projects requiring long-term technical assistance. The Mission has insights, objectives and leverage, which can be applied to the host country government as well as to the institution (if there is a development institution providing the field team) responsible for the technical assistance. It is inappropriate for AID to abdicate its role either to the host country Project Manager or to the technical assistance team leader.

In order for USAID to perform this role, Missions must place greater priority on implementation. If implementation were considered the critical component of AID's activities and could command the attention of its senior staff, this balancing role could be performed in a manner that would guide the project forward on its charted course. In Zaire, DAI, USAID and the host government are still in the formative stages of the project. It is too early to have resolved the difficulties of direction, collaboration and control. During this critical period the contractor can recommend, but AID must act to ensure implementation arrangements that will allow the project to proceed. In spite of years of funding development projects, there are few guidelines or recommendations on how a foreign assistance "middleman" can most effectively promote implementation.

NOTES

[1] The date of project implementation start-up is not always clear. Signing of a Project Agreement is sometimes seen as the beginning of implementation. In a grant and loan program, the grant may be signed long before the terms of the loan are agreed upon and signed. Even after the loan is signed, which we take as the starting point for the project funding disbursement clock, the host country implementing agency may delay implementation until its budget period allows the additional staff and funding to make the project go. In Colombia, USAID considers the start-up date to be the date of the certification of completion of the Conditions Precedent written into the Project Agreement, while the implementing agency sees it as after the implementation plan and agreement with the USAID project officer over the work to be undertaken were completed. Conditions Precedent were met in October 1976, while the implementation planning was completed by January 1, 1977.

[2] After the PRP was completed, but before the Rural Development Specialist arrived, the Provincial Committee closed down the well-staffed and funded operations of the Save the Children Foundation, expelled the American in charge, and confiscated all vehicles and supplies. This U.S. voluntary agency had been working under the auspices of the RRC, without the coordination

or approval of the Provincial Committee.

[3] See, for example, Graham Allison, "Implementation Analysis: 'The Missing Chapter' in Conventional Analysis. A Teaching Experience," in *Benefit-Cost and Policy Analysis* 1974, ed. by Richard Zackhauser et al., Chicago: Aldine Publishing Company, 1975, pp. 369-391.

[4] When technical assistance is loan funded, thus requiring repayment, the recipient is often reluctant to expend monies on foreign advisors. In the Chile project, grant-funded technical assistance was eliminated from the project during the PRP (Interim Report) review on the grounds that Chile, with its relatively high per capita income base, should not receive grant-funded technical assistance. Since this happened after the Colombian episode described earlier, and the consequences of loan-funded technical assistance were by then clear (i.e., none would be used), USAID/Santiago sought a way to fund the necessary assistance through AID's Technical Assistance Bureau, in the same manner that project design support had been funded.

[5] The PRP Team was headed by DAI; however, the Mini-PP and the Project Agreement were written by the Mission and REDSO/EA. The spelling changes in the text for Gemu/Gamu/Gamo Gofa reflect both an official change in name since the PRP was completed, and the complete lack of standardized transliteration from the Amharic language. The official seal of the Provincial Development Office spells it "Gamo Goffa" Province.

[6] At the top of the organization of the Province in socialist Ethiopia is a policy committee, which at this period was called the Provincial Revolutionary Administration and Development Committee; the Province Administrator is the number two ranking official behind the military officer, who is the direct representative of the country's ruling body.

[7] Memorandum from Dr. Jerry Silverman, Arba Minch, Ethiopia, to Donald Mickelwait, DAI/Washington, November 1, 1977.

[8] Morrison-Maierle, an engineering firm located in Helena, Montana, provided four of the ten positions under subcontract to DAI. A women's rural development advisor was added to the team by October 15, 1977, and a research/extension specialist in June 1978. DAI also found it necessary to hire a pilot, since regular flights to the project area were curtailed.

[9] Team members were willing to travel to but not relocate in the project area because of the absence of radio contact to permit emergency medical evacuations, as well as the lack of transportation, and housing with water free of schistosomiasis contamination (which in Kongolo means electricity to supply the

town's water). When arrangements were finally made for radio communications, some housing shells, and a minimal supply of uncontaminated water, those team members without families transferred to Kongolo. An additional problem has been that Lubumbashi was not considered sufficiently secure and stable for families without at least one male team member present. The delays in moving to the project area that resulted from these considerations have produced criticism from the Zairois project staff, who have been living under the conditions that the U.S. team would not accept.

[10] The system was modified in September 1978 under a new Zairois project manager when a local currency fund was established.

[11] This is not to say that the international transfer of money between DAI/Washington and DAI/Lubumbashi is uncomplicated. Transfers from the U.S. require more than five weeks to arrive in an account in Lubumbashi. A transfer back from Lubumbashi, from an account never converted into local currency, disappeared into an international currency exchange crisis. The DAI account was debited in the Lubumbashi bank and a telex was sent to the New York branch of the National Bank of Zaire. However, the New York branch reported that the Lubumbashi Bank did not have sufficient foreign exchange and they would not honor the money transfer. For six weeks $20,000 were missing, until the dollar balance of the Lubumbashi Bank was restored.

[12] The competitive bidding system has had the effect of discouraging continuity. Some of the problems associated with competitive bidding restrictions have been overcome by AID in entering into special arrangements with universities and minority businesses, permitting project designers to continue into implementation.

[13] The "we can do it ourselves" approach and the dedication of the Ethiopians in the project area to make fundamental changes in their economic and political power structure -- in direct support of AID's "New Directions" philosophy -- is impressive and may be worth the short-term delays caused by inadequate technical support.

5 Synthesis and Analysis

The first four chapters have investigated the case histories of twelve rural development projects designed under the "New Directions" mandate of the Agency for International Development. The movement of the projects from identification through implementation has been presented with little analysis, since each activity and stage interrelates with both the preceding and following actions. The purpose here is to produce a qualitative synthesis of the previous chapters. In addition, quantitative "proxies" for success in project design, and the movement through the review and approval process, have been created, and some quantitative analysis has been performed to complement the qualitative work. From an organizational standpoint, it makes most sense to present our qualitative and quantitative findings together by subject. But before doing this, a description of the quantitative work is required. This description follows.

It is clear at the outset that, with only twelve observations, definitive conclusions about success determinants for these projects are not possible. Generalizations about the Agency as a whole would be even less appropriate. However, for projects designed using the process approach, the sample constitutes a relatively large percentage of the total, and the insights may prove valuable to designers who wish to use this same strategy.

Perhaps the most interesting component of this exercise is the attempt to define measures of project design quality and effectiveness of the review/approval process, as well as possible determinants for them.

Ultimately, the only true measure of project success is the effect the project has had on the quality of life of the rural poor.[1] Since only three of the projects under study have entered the implementation stage (and these only barely), nothing is to be gained by developing success measures.

The primary focus of this study is on DAI-assisted design efforts, what happened to them during the AID review/approval process and the implications for implementation. Consequently, three sets of measures have been developed:

- The first involves judgments concerning the quality of project designs as reflected in Project Papers, compared to an ideal design;
- The second involves judgments concerning the effectiveness of the AID review/approval process; and
- The third involves measures that might explain variations in design quality and the effectiveness of review/approval activities.

JUDGING PROJECT DESIGN QUALITY

Two criteria have been developed for the quality of project design. The first compares the actual project design to "ideal" process design requirements. In nine of the twelve projects, DAI attempts to introduce a process approach into project designs were successful. The second involves arriving at some judgments concerning the soundness of the project implementation plan, particularly as it relates to the organizations to be involved in implementation activities. Table 5.1 rates the content of each project, compared to an ideal process approach.

The implementation arrangement judgments (Table 5.2) show two extremes: One in Haiti, where the project is judged unlikely to succeed with the objectives as planned because of a lack of capacity, organization and incentive structure in the implementing agency. The other is the Tanzania Village Development Project, where forceful leadership at the regional level, and a project that fits well into national priorities, make those arrangements an optimum choice.

TABLE 5.1

"IDEAL" PROCESS DESIGN JUDGMENTS

Project	Process Approach Content[a]
Haiti	1
Niger	1
Afghanistan	3
Chile	5
Colombia	5
Ghana	5
Ethiopia	5
Tanzania - FT	5
Tanzania - VD	5
Upper Volta - OP	5
Upper Volta - WP	5
Zaire	5

[a] 1 = low, 5 = high; judged on the basis of a content analysis of the projects against components of the process approach to project design and implementation.

NOTE:

Projects were rated on the basis of the components of the process approach listed on pp. 6-7. A content analysis for each project, on each component of the process approach, was completed by staff members who had not participated in the design. With a summary of the content analysis in hand, the senior DAI designers used their knowledge of the project to provide the final ratings.

TABLE 5.2

PROCESS APPROACH CONTENT
AND IMPLEMENTATION ARRANGEMENTS

Project	Process Approach Content[a]	Implementation Arrangements
Haiti	1	1
Colombia	5	2
Ghana	5	2
Upper Volta - WP	5	2
Zaire	5	2
Afghanistan	3	3
Chile	5	3
Niger	1	3
Tanzania - FT	5	3
Ethiopia	5	4
Upper Volta - OP	5	4
Tanzania - VD	5	5

[a] 5 = high, 1 = low (judged to be poor/inappropriate/unworkable in the case of the implementation arrangements).

NOTE:

Organizational arrangements for implementation were extracted from project documents by DAI staff who had not been part of the design teams. These arrangements were summarized and senior DAI designers used the content analysis item and their knowledge of the project to provide the final rankings.

JUDGING THE EFFECTIVENESS OF THE REVIEW AND APPROVAL PROCESS

Two criteria have been developed for the review/approval process. The first relates to the actual amount of time it took to get projects through the approval process. This time-to-approval variable cannot be assumed to relate directly to the quality of the review/approval process. A long period between Project Paper submission and approval might be the result of a badly designed project that is legitimately returned to the field for major revisions. Unfortunately, there are no clearcut criteria against which to assess the review/approval process involvement in the substance of projects, and this must be kept in mind during the analysis that follows.

The length of time a project is held up in the review process cannot be determined merely by looking at the dates between the last submission and approval, since the delay could (and in the twelve projects did) occur at the PRP or a prior PP stage. After months of wrangling, the PP may be written with no additional information (no further field data collection or analysis), but with a new format or emphasis to satisfy the requirements of the review and approval process. Table 5.3 represents the delays as they have been interpreted under this criterion.

The second criterion examined relates to the efficiency of the review/approval process from the standpoint of decisionmaking. Efficiency of decisionmaking is defined in terms of low decision costs. That is, when a point of disagreement emerges, what does it take, measured in person-weeks of effort, to resolve it? The review/approval process is deemed inefficient when an issue goes back and forth in cables, memos, meetings and other time-consuming activities without resolution. Of course this measure also has its weaknesses. There is no reason to believe that low decision costs automatically mean that good decisions are made.[2] Table 5.4 shows ratings of approval time and review/approval efficiency.

The two scales have eight projects with the same ranking, suggesting that length of time is a useful but not complete proxy for efficiency. The four exceptions are Afghanistan, with a moderate (for the sample) time lag and great rafts of cable and memo traffic, while Tanzania Farmer Training took sixteen months to PP approval with a relatively thin cable/memo file. In terms of demands on the bureaucratic system, it was slow but relatively efficient. Ethiopia struggled with procedural/human rights problems,

TABLE 5.3

PROJECT REVIEW/APPROVAL PROCESS

Project	Documents[a]	Time Elapsed	Codes	Special Circumstances
Tanzania - FT	PRP-2 submission to PP approval	16 months	1	No substantive changes in PRP to PP - All review and approval delays.
Upper Volta - OP	PP submission to approval	15 months	1	
Ghana	PRP-1 to PP approval	13 months	1	All procedural delays - no substantive changes since PRP-1.
Tanzania - VD	PP-1 to approval	12 months	1	"Adequate Planning" delay.
Niger	PP-1 to approval	9 months	3	Major changes in documents as a result of review.
Upper Volta - WP	PP-1 to approval	9 months	3	"Adequate Planning" delay.
Afghanistan	PP-1 to approval	8 months	3	Major changes in review.
Ethiopia	Mini-PP to approval	3 months	5	Human rights
Haiti	PP-1 to approval	2 months	5	
Chile	PP to approval	1 month	5	
Colombia	PP to approval	1 month	5	
Zaire	PP to approval	1 month	5	

1 = Long delays; 5 = rapid approval

[a] Numbers behind the abbreviations refer to the submission sequence. PRP-2 means the second PRP to be submitted; PP-1 means that a second PP was also submitted. (From Table 3.1).

TABLE 5.4

PROJECT REVIEW/APPROVAL RATINGS

Project	Length of Time for Project Review and Approval	Efficiency of Project Review and Approval
Afghanistan	3	1
Ghana	1	1
Niger	1	1
Upper Volta - OP	1	1
Upper Volta - WP	1	1
Ethiopia	5	3
Tanzania - FT	1	3
Chile	5	5
Colombia	5	5
Haiti	5	5
Tanzania - VD	5	5
Zaire	5	5

Code: 1 = low; 5 = high.

NOTE:

The efficiency of the Project Review and Approval process was rated on the thickness of cable and memo traffic in the files, and the actions or activities called for by Missions to satisfy AID/Washington's outstanding requests for such things as more information and changes in project design.

while in Tanzania - VD the adequate planning requirement became a costly concern.

POSSIBLE DETERMINANTS

In order to perform any sort of quantitative analysis on why projects had good or bad designs, or on whether the review/approval process was or was not effective, it was necessary to develop quantitative measures of possible determinants. It was hypothesized that design quality and review/approval process effectiveness depended on DAI involvement (measured in various ways), on host country commitment to the process approach, on host country collaboration during the project design process, and on the size of the project. These variables are precisely defined and presented, along with a correlation matrix for all variables, in an addendum to this chapter.

THE RELATIONSHIP BETWEEN PROJECT QUALITY AND MOVEMENT THROUGH THE REVIEW/APPROVAL PROCESS

A critical question in assessing the effectiveness of the AID review/approval process is whether it discriminates between well and poorly designed projects. An effective review/approval system would presumably stop a badly designed project, or at least force its proponents to take the time and effort to improve the design.

The Review and Approval Process

The review and approval process produced rapid approval in four cases and delays in the other eight projects. Project delays were characterized by:

- Uncertainties in fulfilling the "adequate planning" requirement [611(a)(1)];
- Procedural uncertainties within the approval process;
- Hitches in the system caused by environmental review requirements;
- Disagreements over design methodology (based upon different interpretations of what is needed to promote development)

and over the qualifications of technical assistance personnel; and

- Conflicts over who is to decide which is the most appropriate design methodology. There remained a set of delays from special problems concerning health, international politics, and human rights.

The delays had no apparent consistency between projects within the same Bureau, or among Bureaus. The fluidity of the criteria, as well as the decisionmakers, allows a great deal of personalized interpretation and confusion. Those projects that were not subjected to delays were not better, and could easily be judged worse than some that encountered major setbacks. Finally, the review and approval process made its most apparent impact in the reduction of the efficiency of implementation.

It was possible to do some quantitative analysis on this question. First, an overall quality of project design variable was defined (X_{14}) as the sum of project content (X_1) and implementation arrangements (X_2). An overall measure of the effectiveness of the review/approval process was defined (X_{15}) as being the sum of time-to-approval (X_5) and review/approval efficiency (X_6). A positive correlation would mean high marks for both design and review/approval, i.e., good projects go through fast and bad projects get stalled. A negative correlation would suggest that, for one reason or another, process approach projects are running into serious problems and delays in the review/approval process. An insignificant correlation would suggest randomness in the review/approval process, in the sense that the quality of project design is not a good predictor of what happens at the review/approval stage.

The correlation results agree with the qualitative findings of Chapter 3 that, because of procedural and bureaucratic problems, projects are unnecessarily delayed. There was an insignificant correlation between the design and review/approval variables ($r_{X_{14}, X_{15}} = -.248$).[3] In short, quantitative analysis on this limited sample suggests that the review/approval process is incapable of distinguishing between good and bad project designs.

It is possible that the novelty of the process approach is causing the problem -- that the review/approval process is not geared to evaluate projects employing the "process" approach. If this was the case, a negative correlation should be expected between project content variable (X_1), and the review/approval effectiveness variable (X_{15}). This is not, in fact, the case; there is no correlation between these two variables ($r_{X_1, X_{15}} = -.069$). Alternatively, it is possible that the review/approval process focuses on implementation procedures, i.e., projects with reasonable implementation plans are approved more rapidly. If this were the case, a positive correlation would be expected between the implementation variable (X_2) and the review/approval variable (X_{15}). Here again, the data do not support the hypothesis ($r_{X_2, X_{15}} = -.395$). Indeed, projects that were judged to have more reasonable implementation schemes moved through the review/approval process less effectively!

CONSIDERATIONS IN PROJECT DESIGN

Involvement

The host country commitment to the New Directions concept was of major significance to the completion of an appropriate project design. In Tanzania and Ethiopia the governments have devolved authority to subnational units, providing the basis for province or regional development projects. In turn, the collaboration style was more in evidence -- the governments insisted upon shaping the course of their own development activities and participated in depth in the design activities. Interestingly enough, only in Tanzania in the early months of the New Directions thrust did a Mission not appear to be in agreement with AID/Washington policy directives.

The statistical findings are mixed on this issue. There is no correlation between host country collaboration and quality of project design ($r_{X_{10}, X_{14}} = .124$). However a positive association does exist between host country commitment to the "New Directions" mandate and project quality ($r_{X_8, X_{14}} = .675$).

The low and high rankings on project content (Table 5.1) are straightforward and reflect the degree to which the process approach was a fundamental ingredient of project design. Niger and Haiti, which elected not to use a process approach, rank at the bottom of the twelve projects. In Afghanistan, the middle ranking suggests that the project as approved could be doing more; that is the data base would allow more activity, more testing, more result-oriented development assistance than was approved.

In short this is a judgment that the "start slowly" approach can be carried too far, and minimal provision of an "investigator" with few operational funds is not an appropriate test of the process approach, nor a response to the New Directions mandate.

There should have been positive relationships between resources used by a contractor committed to a team and process approach in the design process, their responsibilities during the design phase, and the extent to which the project reflected the process approach.[4] A one- or two-person team, unless supported by local specialists who are working with a similar philosophy and who take their direction from the senior designer, could not do the job. There were too many unknowns in the local environment, and accepting the views of assorted Mission-selected specialists who were not part of a team approach proved to be an error. As the process approach itself evolved from the early attempts to the later full-blown operations in Ethiopia, Zaire and Tanzania, teams were fielded that included a rural development designer, an anthropologist, agricultural economist and agriculturalists -- requirements which emerged as required for thorough analysis.

The implementation arrangements, even when DAI was heavily involved in the design, often leave a great deal to be desired, when viewed in retrospect. Some of this reflects the real world problems of finding any appropriate and capable Third World government organizations that are up to the task of managing complex development activities. It also reflects the lack of attention, study and concern given this subject in the AID design procedures, and consequently by DAI until well along in the contract.

When any outside consulting organization entered the project in the later stages of project design, the results were less certain than when a fresh slate was available. In four cases a PRP had been completed; in others many different decisions had been made, decisions which should come from the process approach as the project evolves. The already specified dollar target for the project (a creature of the need to obtain prior Congressional notification) caused some over-spending, but was generally reached through the use of infrastructure support in later years of project activities.

Resource Commitment

The total resource commitment for project design has been estimated along with the percentages consumed by the contractor. An interesting question is the relationship between the time used in project design, and the total commitment of AID funds to support the project. Although there is no reason for a relationship to be linear, as there are economies of scale in project design, there might be some common-sense connection, since if project identification includes the target population, a set of goals or objectives, and an implementing agency, a design team can suggest a modest process approach project for relatively low cost. Ten person-weeks would seem to be a good target for a $500,000 project.[5] This would be $50,000 per person-week of design time.

On the other hand, if the New Directions project is to include infrastructure support (as four did) or a large institutional credit component (two projects), a good deal more advance planning is necessary. A useful target for such work is fifty person-weeks, which for a $5,000,000 project would be $100,000 per person-week of design time.

Eliminating the extremes in Table 5.5 as special cases (with Afghanistan, Ethiopia and Ghana all small learn-to-do-it projects) the range is from fifty-four person-weeks in Chile, at nearly $50,000 per person-week in AID funds committed to twelve person-weeks in Tanzania - FT, at over $200,000 per person-week in AID funds committed. It is reasonable for the amount of resource design time to increase with project size. As it turns out there is a positive relationship between the two.[6]

However, there is no correlation between the judgments on project quality and the average per person-week project funding totals. This is presented in Table 5.6, which aggregates the two success ratings into a single score, to compare with the design time/funding average. If improved project quality is not an outcome of increased design time, it is likely that design resources are committed to satisfy the requirements of the review/approval process.

Implementation

It was during implementation that the inadequacies in project design, as well as the review and approval process, became most evident. The first concern was the most appropriate organizational arrangement for implementation. An optimum solution must be determined for each individual project and environment. All solutions used in the cases under review had their limitations, although the subnational

TABLE 5.5

PROJECT FUNDS APPROVED RELATIVE TO DESIGN EFFORT

Project	Total Person-Weeks Spent on Design[a]	Total Funds Approved	Total Funds Approved per Person-Week Design Time	Special Circumstances
Afghanistan	29.2	$ 80,000	$ 2,740	Original Design Eliminated
Ethiopia	30.2	197,000	6,523	Pre-implementation Project
Ghana	19.1	500,000	26,178	
Upper Volta -WP	21.6	1,056,000	48,889	
Upper Volta - OP	24.8	2,173,000	87,621	
Tanzania - FT	12.2	2,514,150	206,078	PRP's Rejected
Chile	54.0	2,600,000	48,148	
Colombia	22.1	3,400,000	153,846	
Niger	26.4	4,699,000	177,992	
Zaire	54.2	9,200,000	169,741	Significant Other Design Effort
Haiti	62.4	12,100,000	193,910	
Tanzania - VD	(41.4)	(14,660,000)	(354,106)	Redesign Work Ongoing

[a] See Table 1.4 (page 34) for the definition of design time.

TABLE 5.6

SUCCESS, TIME-TO-DESIGN AND PROJECT FUNDING LEVELS

Project	Success Scale[a] Sum of Process Approach Content and Implementation Arrangements	Approximate Total Funds Approved Per Person-Week Design Time[b]
Tanzania - VD	10	$ 355,000
Upper Volta - OP	9	90,000
Ethiopia	9	5,000
Tanzania - FT	8	205,000
Chile	8	50,000
Zaire	7	170,000
Upper Volta - WP	7	50,000
Ghana	7	25,000
Colombia	7	150,000
Afghanistan	6	5,000
Niger	4	175,000
Haiti	2	195,000

---

[a] Derived from Table 5.2.

[b] Derived from Table 5.5.

governments, in countries where real power and authority has been delegated below the national level, would be the first choice. Working through line ministries at the national level generated the tradeoff between an existing institution, and an overly narrow focus on traditional agricultural activities. If the subnational governments are not given authority, or listened to by national planners (as they may not be in Ghana), such an arrangement will produce little more than frustration in a district planning office. Integrated development agencies at the national level run the risk of direct confrontation with more traditional ministries, while special project management units, because of the finite nature of their existence (while the need to generate self-sustaining development remains) were considered a last choice for an implementing organization. The complex requirements and the lack of guidelines in the field of development administration should be one of the major concerns of project design teams. That it is not, and was not in the cases studied, reflects a poor understanding of the implementation process in prior AID design procedures.

The need for implementation analysis was set forth in the three projects currently undergoing implementation. Five major problem areas were listed, but these hardly exhaust the difficulties encountered in attempting to move from design into actual operations. Most of the problems could be overcome if the time and attention of the most capable AID staff were devoted to making implementation effective. Because of the necessity to satisfy the AID/Washington review and approval process prior to obtaining funds, field staffs concentrate on project design (and Congressional budget presentations and similar requirements), while leaving implementation support to lower ranking, non-policy officials.

Proper implementation requires a very close balancing of the technical assistance team (when one is required) and the host country implementing agency. The analysis suggests that USAID project officers need adroit footwork, excellent policy leadership, and a sound knowledge of the potential pitfalls of project operations before they can effectively fulfill this role. In the present environment of AID, with the low priority and little emphasis on the problems of implementation, this is too much to expect.

SUMMARY

The three projects that scored lowest on project quality (Table 5.6) are those where there were major miscommunications or disagreements between the design team and one of the other parties (Mission field staff or AID/Washington). Of the high-ranked projects, two (Tanzania - VD and Ethiopia) are still in the beginning process of implementation. This has the potential to make them even better, as in Ethiopia where pre-implementation is ongoing, or worse, as in Tanzania where a procedural problem with the adequate planning requirement delayed implementation start-up.

The remaining well-designed projects -- Upper Volta - OP,[7] Tanzania - FT and Chile -- are those where the Mission and host country were involved in the planning and design, although the Tanzania - FT project has undergone major changes since DAI involvement.

Reviewing the projects and the judgments on content and implementation arrangements, it appears that high marks were more easily obtained when:

- There was a strong host country commitment to AID's New Directions (Tanzania and Ethiopia);

- The process approach philosophy entered the project very early in the design phase, and did not encounter a competing Mission or contract team appproach;

- The process approach team, which included a Mission representative, collected and analyzed data, tested hypotheses, and formulated basic design concepts with the principal actors at all levels in the host country, who would be responsible for implementation;

- The implementation arrangements were given equal priority with the design components necessary to involve and benefit the small farmers and rural poor; and as a corollary,

- Implementation could be stronger when the technical assistance was furnished by the institution that generated the design for the project with "home office" involvement and commitment to make the project work.

NOTES

1 For some operational attempts to develop ultimate success measures for projects, see *Strategies* report, op. cit., pp. 20-26.

2 See Chapter 9 for an analysis of this point.

3 This correlation coefficient is not significant at the ninety-five percent level for twelve observations.

4 The quantitative analysis is mixed on these assertions. There is no correlation between the level of DAI resources and the extent to which the project design reflects the process approach ($r_{X_1, X_3} = .164$). However, there is a high positive correlation between the quality of the implementation plan and the comprehensiveness of the DAI involvement ($r_{X_2, X_9} = .641$).

5 This calculation excludes the packaging for Washington review and approval, which is estimated to consume fifty percent of most design team activities. Ghana, with a small half-million dollar project designed in twenty actual person-weeks (ten ideal), is an example of the modest project design.

6 This refers to Columns 1 and 2 of Table 5.5, a correlation which was omitted from the statistical addendum to this chapter.

7 The Oncho project in Upper Volta ran into difficulty establishing health criteria late in project review. This can be viewed as a review process operating efficiently to catch a poor project design. It could also be concluded that the project was well designed, since the outcome of the health review changed only the health criteria to be used to ensure that the area was oncho-free.

ADDENDUM TO CHAPTER FIVE

Definitions of Variables Included in Quatitative Analysis

X_1 A scale indicating the extent to which the final project proposal reflects the "process" approach. High numbers on the (1-5) scale indicate a close correspondence to the process approach. The scale was developed from the content analyses used in developing Table 5.1.

X_2 A scale reflecting the reasonableness of the organizational arrangements for project implementation, as seen at the time of project approval. High values on this (1-5) scale reflect judgments by DAI that the organizational arrangements were sound (Table 5.2).

X_3 DAI involvement in project design, as measured in person-weeks (Table 1.4).

X_4 DAI involvement in project design, as a percent of the total person-weeks of effort that went into project design. (This figure was derived from Table 1.4.)

X_5 A scale reflecting the time for initial project to project approval, with high values on the (1-5) scale reflecting short approval times. In the case of Ghana the PRP is used, since it was submitted as the PP behind a face sheet. Tanzania - VD time to approval is estimated as March 1978 (Table 5.4).

X_6 This (1-5) scale is intended to reflect the efficiency of the approval process, where efficiency is defined as the amount of time spent reaching decisions in the review/approval process. It is not a measure of the time-lapse between submission and approval, but rather the time spent, as reflected in cable traffic and other available information, in attempting to resolve issues. A high value reflects an efficient decision process in the sense that issues were resolved with little back-and-forth argumentation (Table 5.4).

X_7 This (1-5) scale reflects the extent to which DAI participated in the AID/Washington review/approval process. A high value indicates a high degree of participation.

X_8 A scale reflecting, in the judgment of DAI staff, host country commitment to AID's "New Directions." A high score reflects a high commitment (Table 1.2).

X_9 A scale representing the number of steps DAI was involved in. The steps include: design, working-level collaboration with host country counterparts, negotiations with host country decisionmakers, packaging for approval, and data for justification. The (1-5) scale represents the number of steps in which DAI was involved (derived from Table 1.5).

X_{10} A (1-5) scale of the commitment of the host country officials at the national level collaborated in the design effort. A high value represents a high level of collaboration (derived from Table 2.3).

X_{11} A (1-5) scale of the commitment of the host country implementing agency to the project as designed. A high score reflects high commitment (Table 2.3).

X_{12} Total AID funds approved for the project (Table 5.5).

X_{13} Total AID funds approved for the project (X_{12}), divided by total person-weeks spent on design (Table 1.4). This is a funds-obligated-per-person-week-design-time variable.

X_{14} The sum of X_1 and X_2.

X_{15} The sum of X_5 and X_6.

TABLE 5.7

DATA FOR QUANTITATIVE ANALYSIS

	Design				Review/Approval		
Project	Content	Implementation	DAI Person-Weeks	DAI Percent of Total Person-Weeks	Timing	Efficiency	DAI Review/Approval Participation
	x_1	x_2	x_3	x_4	x_5	x_6	x_7
Afghanistan	3	3	22.6	77.4	3	1	3
Chile	5	3	42.0	77.8	5	5	3
Colombia	5	2	2.6	11.8	5	5	1
Ethiopia	5	4	11.2	37.0	5	3	5
Ghana	5	2	10.1	52.9	1	1	3
Haiti	1	1	8.4	13.5	5	5	1
Niger	1	3	5.4	20.5	3	1	1
Tanzania-FT	5	3	5.2	42.6	1	3	3
Tanzania-VD	5	5	11.4	27.5	3	1	5
Upper Volta-OP	5	4	10.8	43.5	1	1	1
Upper Volta-WP	5	2	15.6	72.2	3	1	1
Zaire	5	2	11.3	20.8	5	5	5

TABLE 5.7 (Continued)

Project	Host Country Commitment to New Directions	Comprehensiveness of DAI Involvement	National-Level Collaboration	Commitment of Implementing Agency to Project as Designed	Total AID Funds Approved for the Project	Total AID Funds Per Person-Week of Design Time
	x_8	x_9	x_{10}	x_{11}	x_{12}	x_{13}
Afghanistan	3	4	3	1	$ 80,000	2,740
Chile	3	3	5	5	2,600,000	48,148
Colombia	3	2	1	1	3,400,000	153,846
Ethiopia	5	5	5	5	197,000	6,523
Ghana	3	3	1	1	500,000	26,178
Haiti	1	1	1	1	12,100,000	193,910
Niger	3	5	5	3	4,699,000	177,992
Tanzania-FT	5	4	1	1	2,514,150	206,078
Tanzania-VD	5	5	1	5	(14,660,000)	(354,106)
Upper Volta-OP	3	5	5	5	2,173,000	87,621
Upper Volta-WP	3	5	1	3	1,056,000	48,889
Zaire	1	5	5	3	9,200,000	169,741

TABLE 5.8

MATRIX OF CORRELATION COEFFICIENTS

	x_1	x_2	x_3	x_4	x_5	x_6	x_7	x_8	x_9	x_{10}	x_{11}	x_{12}	x_{13}	x_{14}	x_{15}
x_1	1.000														
x_2	0.326	1.000													
x_3	0.164	0.113	1.000												
x_4	0.293	0.114	0.750	1.000											
x_5	-0.160	-0.260	0.242	-0.275	1.000										
x_6	0.020	-0.464	0.134	0.350	0.736	1.000									
x_7	0.435	0.456	0.179	0.030	0.174	0.077	1.000								
x_8	0.414	0.752	-0.064	0.176	-0.353	-0.411	0.353	1.000							
x_9	0.298	0.641	-0.024	0.186	-0.303	-0.574	0.382	0.403	1.000						
x_{10}	-0.048	0.314	0.352	0.078	0.237	0.081	0.200	-0.125	0.458	1.000					
x_{11}	0.329	0.710	0.381	0.121	0.141	-0.126	0.343	0.315	0.580	0.600	1.000				
x_{12}	-0.270	0.037	-0.205	-0.607	0.299	0.258	0.211	-0.232	-0.132	-0.204	0.113	1.000			
x_{13}	-0.144	0.203	-0.422	-0.649	0.007	0.105	0.118	0.104	0.002	-0.322	0.035	0.853	1.000		
x_{14}	0.880	0.736	0.174	0.267	-0.246	-0.219	0.541	0.675	0.536	0.124	0.592	-0.175	-0.000	1.000	
x_{15}	-0.069	-0.395	0.198	-0.337	0.923	0.940	0.132	-0.412	-0.479	0.166	0.000	0.298	0.063	-0.248	1.000

II
Reflections on the Process Approach to Project Development

6 Project Design Issues

Over the course of DAI's design experience, several issues arose with sufficient frequency to warrant discussion. Some of these issues were substantive; others were more procedural in nature. Several revolved around the acceptability of the process approach to project development. All the issues involved different interpretations of what is required to bring development benefits to small farmers.

COMPOSITION OF THE DESIGN TEAM

One issue, which arose early in several of the project design exercises, concerned the type of individuals needed on a project design team. This issue took on several dimensions.

One dimension concerned the source of team members. In most design exercises, representatives from AID and the host country participated. In every case this proved both necessary and desirable. In the case of AID, it proved important to have a participant from the Mission itself (or from REDSO), rather than from AID/Washington; it was also helpful if the participant was scheduled to play some role in the implementation of the project. The most useful sort of host country participant was a responsible member of the organization tapped to implement the project. When the AID participant was from the Mission, and when the host country representative was from the implementing agency, the individuals in question had greater incentives to make the project design a living, workable document that could be implemented, rather than simply a mechanism for transferring funds from Washington to the host country.

When outside consultants were used, it was invariably preferable to put together a team that shared a common approach to development and had a common institutional base, or had at least worked together in the past, rather than assemble individuals whose paper qualifications rated them as experts but who might not be able to work together as a team.[1]

In one project, Niger, DAI provided the design team leader while other team members were provided by universities, Peace Corps and private consultants. The results were so poor that DAI has adopted a corporate policy not to repeat that error. The work of a design team involves field data collection and analysis, the synthesis of information into coherent design, and active collaboration with host country officials and participants. In general, it is not possible to accomplish these tasks with a mixed group, whose members do not share a common approach to development, or may have little concern for the workability of the project.

Another dimension of the issue involves the specialties that are needed on a design team. One approach is to assemble a team composed of individuals with exotic specialties (e.g., range agronomists, water development specialists, animal traction experts) that are seen to fit the demands of the development problem at hand. While such a team may generate a worthwhile project, DAI's experience is that this would be the exception. At least one member of a design team should have sufficient technical background to judge the appropriateness of different technological packages, but the critical skills needed on a design team were found to be not so much technical in nature as those that contribute to a sensible project in a particular political, economic, social and cultural milieu. This requires individuals with a certain breadth of experience in a variety of development situations, and with the personal skills needed to collaborate and negotiate with host country officials.

In most of the design exercises, a core group consisting of a rural development specialist, an anthropologist or rural sociologist, an economist (usually an agricultural economist) and an agriculturalist proved to be effective. It was desirable that at least one member of the core group also have experience and expertise in project management arrangements. In many of the design exercises, the participation of female professionals was found to be not simply desirable but necessary. In Afghanistan for example, local professional women were needed to communicate with village women, and in Zaire village women would not voice their opinions in the presence of men.

The design teams found much of the technical knowledge needed to develop project components available in the host country. Where more detailed study or work was required, this was built into the project design. Experience with technical specialists assigned to design teams was mixed; as a general rule, though, stateside specialists who had little experience in developing countries were unable to apply their knowledge to local conditions in a meaningful way.

EFFICACY OF AN INCOME/PRODUCTION-ORIENTED STRATEGY

AID's Congressional mandate suggests that agency programs should be directed toward improving the quality of life of the rural poor and meeting their basic needs. One possible strategy for achieving these goals is to place priority on projects that provide heavy up-front doses of social services such as education, health, nutrition and shelter. Another strategy is to help poor communities develop a self-sustaining income base so that they might provide or help provide these services for themselves.

Most of the twelve projects had strong income/production orientations. Implicit in this thrust is the assumption that, as local organizational and financial capabilities are developed, the local population will be able to identify and support the social services most needed. Only when illiteracy or poor health constituted critical constraints to the initiation of production/income-oriented activities were these components built into project designs. An example would be the lack of a safe, reliable water supply, which was identified as a constraint in Afghanistan, Ghana, and Upper Volta.

It is not argued here that health, nutritional, and educational services are not needed. The operative questions concern timing and priorities. The *Strategies* report concluded that success in rural development projects was directly related to the willingeness of farmers to commit resources to a development effort, and that willingness to commit resources is affected negatively by the up-front provision of social services. For example, previous development projects in Ghana created unrealistic expectations of services from the government, institutionalizing a strong dependency relationship. A principal objective of an income/production-oriented strategy is to weaken that dependency relationship.

Furthermore, building local financial and organizational capabilities may improve the chances that benefits will become self-sustaining.

This approach argues that, if social services are strongly desired by a rural population, they should be willing to help pay for them. In the DAI-assisted projects, an attempt was made to introduce service programs that required initial resource commitments by the local population and included mechanisms for shifting total costs to the users.

AVAILABILITY AND APPROPRIATENESS OF TECHNOLOGY

Appropriate technology (in the sense of suitability to the immediate environment) is essential for increasing the production and incomes of small farmers. In all twelve projects, it was the judgment of the design teams that the optimal technology was lacking; this view was sometimes strongly disputed by host country and foreign donor technicians. This dichotomy of views was especially evident in situations where considerable resources were being expended to develop and/or introduce small farmer technological packages, as in the National Cereals Program in Niger, the Agricultural Research Project in Tanzania, and the National Maize Program (PNM) in Zaire.

In the design exercises, the first question was whether improved technologies already existed. The answer was almost always positive, with evidence in the form of findings of research institutes and, in some cases, field trials. The second question (and first source of conflict) was whether the available technology was appropriate for the environment of the development project. The answer to this question hinges on these issues:

- Whether the technology is acceptable to small farmers, given their existing farming systems and their perception of the risks entailed in changing current practices; and

- Whether the agricultural support system is capable of providing services and supplies on a correct and timely basis.

The issue of technology choice becomes complex when considered from the viewpoint of small farmers.

Whereas agriculturalists generally seek to maximize yields, and economists normally seek to maximize expected income, the first concern of the subsistence farmer is to maximize the chances of earning a subsistence income. Only when this is assured will they possibly consider additional income possibilities.[2] The difference between benefit-cost results obtained at research stations (where the risk to the farmer is not a primary concern), and the benefit-cost relationship as perceived by farmers, is often great.

The key factor is "the cost of risk," which a farmer perceives as a valid cost, while researchers or extension workers frequently do not. If a research station experiment fails, the researcher has merely lost an experiment; if a farmer fails, his entire livelihood may be jeopardized. Reduction of risk is therefore the first criterion that the new technology must meet. If this is satisfied, the new technology should sooner or later cover its costs. All increases in production costs attributable to the new technology must be fully covered by the gains from the increased yields.

The only way to determine the acceptability of technology to small farmers is to test it on their own lands. While there is normally no dispute over this point, divergent views emerge regarding the best approach for development and testing new technologies. The process approach calls first for an understanding of current farming systems. This understanding provides a foundation for identifying and developing technologies that can be used by small farmers without major changes in behavior and resource commitments. As small farmer technical knowledge and resources expand, more advanced technologies can be introduced.

While more advanced technologies may result in significantly higher yields and income, there remains the question of whether the agricultural support system can provide the necessary inputs to support their introduction. Frequently this entails highly trained local technicians, an effective delivery system of agricultural supplies, and expanded credit and marketing services. Developing an efficient and effective support system requires significant resources, especially if petrochemical products are needed. Before such advanced technologies are introduced to small farmers, it must be determined whether a reliable agricultural support system can be developed and maintained after foreign donor resources are withdrawn.

An Illustration of the Issue: Zaire

These complex considerations concerning the appropriateness of available technology emerged in full force during the design of the Zaire North Shaba Project. The Government of Zaire places a very high priority on attaining national self-sufficiency in the supply of maize and has established the National Maize Program (PNM), which is currently staffed by a group of U.S.- and CIMMYT-trained plant scientists. These scientists have developed technological packages for maize growing that involve improved seeds and cultivation practices, small amounts of fertilizer, and pure strand production. Under the project, the PNM was to test and introduce the new technology.

The design team's field investigations showed that there were several distinct ecological zones in the project area, with different farming systems being employed in each zone. It also determined that the agricultural supplies and credit were almost nonexistent, that the communications and logistical systems were in total disrepair, and that the marketing system could not handle the existing supply of maize. Furthermore, the government was suffering a serious balance of payments problem. Yet even under these conditions, the PNM (with the guidance of CIMMYT advisors) was prepared to argue that the available technology was appropriate and should be utilized in the project.

The solution in the Zaire project design was to use the process approach to identify immediate (short-term) interventions while initiating the testing of the PNM technological packages. It was recognized that time was an important factor for technology development and for creation of an agricultural support system. Sufficient flexibility was built into the project so that resources would be available if conditions improved and if the more advanced technology proved acceptable to farmers. Effective implementation of the solution will require a reorientation of PNM personnel from a largely agronomic frame of reference to that of the small farmer, including his perception of the risk of relying on the government's agricultural support system.

Applicability of the Zaire Solution

The Zaire solution appears suitable for countries with similar difficulties. Modifications in the approach are needed, however, in countries where more advanced technologies are already in use and the agricultural support system is more fully developed. In such cases there is a need to develop mechanisms, such as the farm records system created for the Chile project, so that the farmers have the information necessary to decide which technologies to use. Such information and farmer feedback are also needed to assist in the adaptation of intermediate and advanced technologies to local conditions.

THE "BOTTOM-UP" APPROACH AND NATIONAL/REGIONAL PLANNING

"Bottom-up" approaches to project development are often criticized on the grounds that they give insufficient attention to those regional and national macro-policies that affect local-level development. Ideally, the process of learning about an area and testing alternatives will enable development workers to formulate recommendations to improve national and regional systems in ways that support local development. At the most elementary level, for example, the process should yield specific insights about which elements of the national agricultural support system need to be improved in order to serve small farmers effectively. Another possibility would be the identification of important links in the region's road system that need to be rehabilitated or constructed. Beyond identifying possible inputs from the national and regional levels, this approach can also develop farmers' economic resources so that they can invest in area development, helping to increase the chances for benefits to become self-sustaining. Many larger questions may loom on the horizon, however, and the process approach is not tied to a political philosophy that prescribes solutions to macro-level political problems. In this sense it falls short of being a remedy for all the ills of underdevelopment. But it can strengthen the voice of small farmers, who have all too often been "silent partners" in what should be a dialogue with decisionmakers in the upper tiers of a political/administrative hierarchy. In making their voices heard, populations become subjects rather than objects (or "targets") of development.

Each of the twelve projects encountered a different set of structural relationships affecting the possibilities of promoting a bottom-up dialogue. The precedents for such a dialogue were far more encouraging in Tanzania, for example, than in Zaire or Afghanistan. In the most strongly centralized political environments, the designers had to recognize that attuning national-level officials to respond to local initiatives is a complex process: it entails preparing them to both "listen to" and "hear" what members of the rural population have to say about their development needs and capabilities.

THE PROCESS APPROACH AND PRESSURES FOR IMMEDIATE ACTION

There are considerable pressures on AID Missions to spend money, and on host country development agencies to produce results rapidly. However, the process approach required in almost every case an initial period of information collection and adaptive field-testing, laying a solid foundation for self-sustaining development, and not putting too great a strain on fragile systems by attempting to do too much too rapidly. Design teams were, therefore, faced with the dilemma of attempting to reconcile the potential conflict between the process approach and the perceived need of these agencies to commit resources. Solutions to this problem had to fit the circumstances of project and country.

One solution (in Zaire) was the early identification of heavy infrastructure requirements and the basic needs of the agricultural support system. Procurement of equipment and full development of these programs would require time, so that an evolutionary process could still operate in the project as a whole. In addition, sufficient flexibility was built into the project so that resources could be redirected as new insights were gained during the implementation experience.

Another solution was found in the Tanzania Village Development Project. The information system's functions at the local level are directly tied into the overall regional planning effort. This provides a strong foundation for developing a sound plan, based on the realities of different parts of the region. Nonetheless problems remain in determining what combination of development resources and activities is needed at each level, local and national or regional, to ensure self-sustaining developmental change.

NOTES

[1] An analogy can be made to the mixed group of individualist stars on the Philadelphia 76ers and the coherent team known as the Portland Trailblazers. Basketball fans know that the

Trailblazers beat the 76ers for the national championship in 1977.

[2] Development Alternatives, Inc., *Small Farmer Risk-Taking*, prepared for the Rural Development Office, TAB, AID, June 1976.

7
The Role of "Experimentation" in Development Projects

INTRODUCTION

In discussing the twelve projects, frequent reference has been made to the need for flexibility and the "experimental" nature of proposed project activities. This reflects a principal thesis of the process approach to project development, that appropriate interventions must be identified through systematic testing in field situations. In the documentation reviewed for this report, several projects were explicitly described as "experiments." The purpose of this chapter is to describe the sorts of "experimentation" that are possible in rural development projects.

It is important to distinguish between two definitions of "experimentation" at the project level:

- The project as an experiment to test one or more specific hypotheses within a given time frame, where the analysis consists of comparing the salient features of the project area with untreated "control" areas; or

- A dynamic, ongoing process where the project serves as a time-and-resource framework for systematic testing and application of techniques identified as appropriate to local conditions. The outcome is a methodology that can be replicated in other comparable (but not necessarily equivalent) situations, enabling similar projects to be developed on the basis of knowledge accumulated during the implementation experience.

The first definition is consistent with the procedures of classical social experimentation. It implies a degree of rigor and precision that is rarely, if ever, achieved in the context of a development project. The second definition, which conveys the spirit and meaning of the process approach, corresponds much more closely to actual and potential practice in project situations.

It would seem, on the basis of this distribution, that the concepts of *adaptive research* and *field-testing of interventions* more accurately capture the thrust of the process approach than *social experimentation*. In this regard the DAI involvement in designing the twelve projects has led to a better understanding of what is required in actually practicing flexibility, as opposed to merely preaching it. In the following discussion, the standard terminology of social experimentation is used only in quotes in order to avoid confusion.

REVIEW OF THE PROJECTS' "EXPERIMENTAL" CONTENT

In almost every case, DAI's contribution to the twelve projects emphasized that "unknown" factors bearing on project implementation had to be investigated. Significantly, this analysis did not entail delaying implementation until all of the outstanding questions had been answered. On the contrary, it was argued that predicting social dynamics is difficult, that design and implementation are actually inseparable, and that "unknowns" can be best identified and dealt with through interaction with small farmers. The process of project development would therefore involve systematically reducing the "unknowns" or, in other words, finding answers where none had existed at the start. These answers, it should be noted, would take the form of workable and cost-effective intervention techniques, rather than abstract theoretical formulations.

As explained elsewhere in this report, the specific attention to "unknowns" (focusing on possible constraints to project success), as opposed to predetermined solutions (already "proven" in other contexts and thus assumed to offer a guarantee of success), represented a radical departure from conventional approaches to project development.

The nature and extent of the "unknowns" varied, of course, from one design assignment to another. As Figure 7.1 shows, there were situations where a strong preexisting data base was supplemented by the design team, using rapid survey techniques: the two Upper Volta projects present the clearest examples of this strategy. On the other side of the coin, for example in the Ethiopia and Afghanistan assignments, there were situations characterized by the almost total absence of preexisting, locally generated data. Thus variability in the knowledge base was one determinant of how and at what level it was proposed to begin implementation.

The conceptual paradigm of project development using the process approach incorporates the following elements:

- Improving knowledge of the social system and the production environment;
- Establishing a range of possible interventions;
- Testing the possible interventions;
- Using test results to identify interventions appropriate to the local context;
- Applying interventions in a way that will distribute their benefits within the project area; and
- Replicating the project methodology in comparable target areas.

The logical sequence could be described, in simple terms, as Research-Experimentation-Action-Replication. The progression is not strictly linear, however: research and testing do <u>not</u> stop where application and replication begin. More accurately, the relationship should be thought of as cyclical, with the results of field tests being fed back into the redesign of project activities: This has been represented in Figure 7.1.

It is also useful to distinguish between two types of orientation manifested in the documentation of the twelve projects:

- An evolutionary orientation, with a gradual build-up of activities (and associated increases in funding) through more or less clearly delineated phases; or
- An orientation that presumes that these activities can be initiated more or less concurrently.

With respect to this orientation criterion, the projects can be broken down in the following fashion:

FIGURE 7.1

PROJECT DEVELOPEMENT FLOW CHART

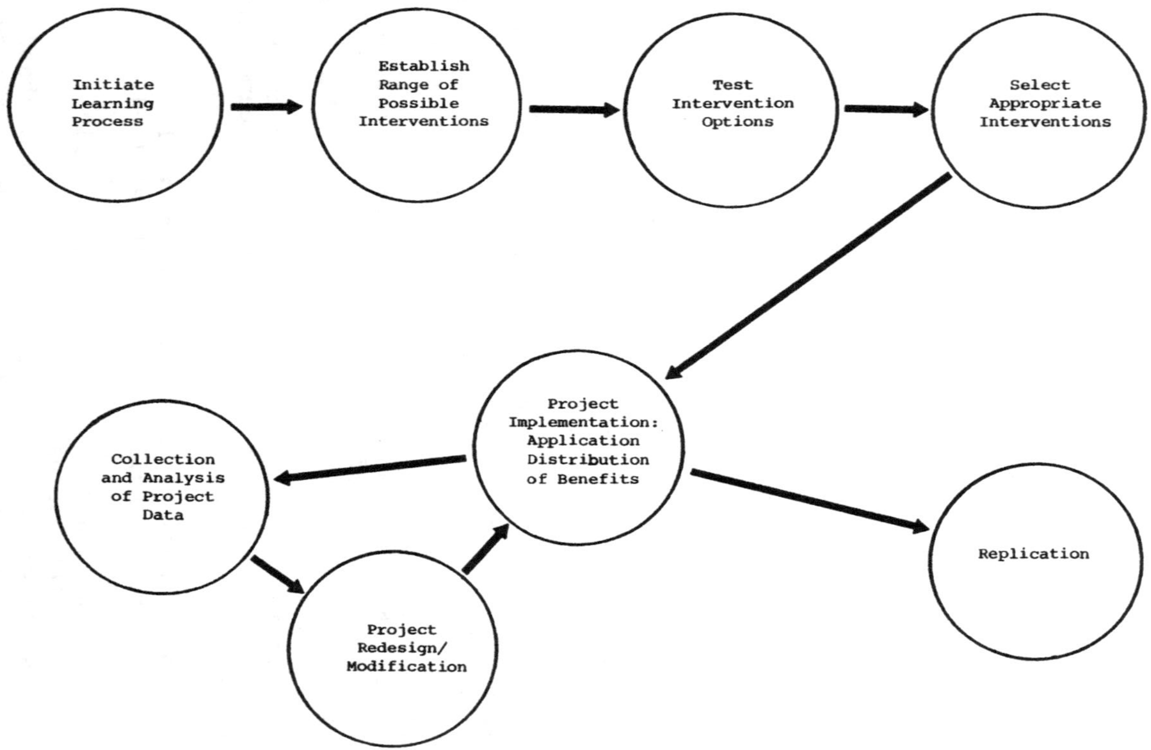

Evolutionary	Concurrent
Ghana	Upper Volta - OP
Ethiopia	Upper Volta - WP
Zaire	Chile
Afghanistan	Tanzania - FT
Colombia	Niger (B)
Tanzania - VD	Haiti (B)
Niger (A)	
Haiti (A)	

The Niger and Haiti projects reflect sharply conflicting interpretations of what was required: (A) in each instance represents the project design just after DAI final input, while (B) represents the final outcome of design (in the case of Niger, a revised PP, and in the case of Haiti, a PP written without continuing DAI participation). Indeed, both Niger (B) and Haiti (B) virtually eliminated all "experimental" or testing activities proposed in the (A) versions, abandoning the process approach in favor of supposedly "proven" interventions.

The fact that the final versions of half the projects do not fit the evolutionary category can be attributed to several factors. In addition to the variation in the knowledge base, as already suggested, both host country preferences (typically insistence on an "action" component with some immediate impact on the target population, i.e., visible results within a very short timeframe) and AID preferences (particularly an unwillingness to fund "research") have a direct impact on the shape of the final design and the amount of testing activity that can be built into it. In Chile, for example, host country policies called for a program based in the private sector that would distribute sufficient benefits to allow participating farmers to pay for services received. In the Niger and Haiti cases, DAI staff and AID personnel were in strong disagreement about whether any "research" activities were needed at all.

In terms of project content, the "experimental" features can be summarized in a matrix that facilitates cross-project comparisons. This matrix (Figure 7.2) has been constructed for all projects except Niger and Haiti. The three analytical categories used are: principal unknowns, as perceived by the design team; adaptive research requirements to be satisfied during project implementation; and procedural outcome of each research activity (the methodological output). The enumeration of the latter two categories has been matched with the project

FIGURE 7.2

FIELD-TESTING CONTENT OF PROCESS APPROACH PROJECTS

	Principal "Unknowns"	Adaptive Research Requirements	Procedural Outcome
GHANA	Complexity of small farmer social and production systems.	1. Reduction of major unknowns.	1. Narrows range of potential interventions.
	Lack of experience in effectively reaching the rural poor.	2. Test District Council's ability to initiate and structure activities.	2. Provides a basis for planning procedures at District level.
		3. Test new agricultural technology and methods of knowledge transfer.	3. Aids technology selection and specifies effective extension approach.
		4. Test options for new small-scale rural enterprises.	4. Identifies promising types of village enterprises.
		5. Test labor-intensive small public works.	5. Identifies means of mobilizing self-help and resource commitment.
		6. Test local employment potential through non-formal education.	6. Provides basis for design of training and non-formal education.
		7. Test utility of data types and sources in information system.	7. Identifies critical categories of data and their uses.
ETHIOPIA	Highly complex local social and economic systems.	1. Identify major agricultural production constraints, needs.	1. Narrows range of potential interventions.
	Appropriate technologies not yet available.	2. Identify livestock production constraints and needs.	2. Narrows range of potential interventions.
	Training needs of newly-formed peasant associations not determined.	3. Test sources of water and potential delivery systems.	3. Narrows range of potential interventions.
		4. Test prototype small-scale enterprises.	4. Narrows range of interventions to most viable options.
		5. Test new methods of training for village-based workers.	5. Provides basis for developing full-scale training program.
		6. Identify data needs and methods of collection.	6. Identifies critical categories of data and their uses.

	Principal "Unknowns"	Adaptive Research Requirements	Procedural Outcome
ZAIRE	Dearth of information on small farmer behavior and constraints. Differences in decision-making patterns between areas not well understood. Methods of enlisting cooperation and participation not yet known.	1. Test innovations and alternatives in crop production. 2. Establish provisional farmer groups in 75 localities. 3. Test equipment for production, processing and storage. 4. Test policies and activities to develop private sector marketing capabilities. 5. Set up new local brigade for road construction. 6. Test utility of data sources and types for project decisionmakers.	1. Generates criteria for identifying best techniques. 2. Helps to determine basis of organization for farmer groups. 3. Permits selection of technology appropriate to local conditions. 4. Identifies training and resource inputs needed to develop local marketing services. 5. Identifies means of mobilizing self-help and resource commitment. 6. Identifies critical categories of data and utility for ongoing modification of project.
UPPER VOLTA (OP)	Inadequate understanding of acceptability and profitability and other income-generating activities. Absence of longstanding basis for intra-village cooperation and organization.	1. Test various types of village enterprises. 2. Innovative interaction methodologies between project staff and villagers used in training. 3. Information system to test efficacy of village enterprises and organizations.	1. Generates criteria for identifying most promising village enterprises. 2. Helps to identify most effective methods of training villagers and extension staff. 3. Identifies critical categories of data and uses in decisionmaking.
UPPER VOLTA (WP)	Lack of experience with programs capable of involving women in economic production activities.	1. Revolving loan funds to support micro-projects on trial basis. 2. Test methods of improving technical and management skills of female extension workers and village leaders. 3. Information system to develop proxy indicators of village-level development.	1. Generates criteria for identifying replicable and self-sustaining women's activities. 2. Helps to identify ways of expanding women's involvement in extension activities. 3. Identifies critical categories of data and uses in decisionmaking.

FIGURE 7.2 (Continued)

	Principal "Unknowns"	Adaptive Research Requirements	Procedural Outcome
TANZANIA (OP)	Small farmers' production constraints and decision-making not well understood. Little known about behavior change or acceptability of new technologies.	1. Test alternative methods of transferring knowledge through extension. 2. Field-testing of technological packages. 3. Testing of data collection instruments and information needs.	1. Identifies most effective methods of training extension staff and villagers. 2. Permits selection of technologies appropriate to local conditions. 3. Identifies critical categories of data and uses in decisionmaking.
TANZANIA (VD)	Methods of planning from the village up not yet known. Insufficient data base on small farmers' production constraints.	1. Testing of methods to promote local level planning capacity. 2. Testing and diffusion of technological innovations and alternatives. 3. Testing of technologies for small-scale enterprises.	1. Identifies methods and procedures for effective planning at local and regional levels. 2. Aids in selection of environmentally sound and appropriate technologies. 3. Identifies promising acitivities suited to particular micro-level environments.
COLOMBIA	Research station technologies not ready for wide promotion. Effective means of extension to small farmers not determined. Trends in small farm productivity not well understood.	1. Investigation of major "unknowns" and constraints. 2. Adaptive research on promising production technologies. 3. Diffusion and further testing of results from 2. 4. Test capacity of local organizations. 5. Test methods and instruments of data collection, develop proxy indicators.	1. Narrows range of potential interventions. 2. Permits selection of technologies appropriate to local conditions. 3. Identifies most effective system of knowledge transfer among farmers. 4. Helps identify most viable types of local organizations. 5. Identifies critical categories of data and their uses.

	Principal "Unknowns"	Adaptive Research Requirements	Procedural Outcome
AFGHANISTAN	Weak knowledge base in almost all areas of social and economic systems.	1. Test alternative planning procedures at district level.	1. Generates criteria for increasing planning capacity at district level.
	Uncertainty about modes of entry for intervention in local communities.	2. Test alternatives and innovations in water availability, distribution arrangements, and on-farm use.	2. Helps to identify most appropriate intervention techniques to improve production and income.
		3. Test alternative organizational bases for village-level decision-making.	3. Helps to identify ways of introducing interventions into local communities.
		4. Information system to test data collection instruments and methods.	4. Identifies critical categories of data and their uses in decision-making.
CHILE	Capacity of paratechnicians for extension and data gathering unproven.	1. Testing of linked credit/extension package by Farm Management Unit.	1. Identifies suitable financial and organizational basis for extension system in land reform sector.
	Absence of field-tested appropriate technologies.	2. Identification of promising technological alternatives and innovations.	2. Aids in selection of technologies appropriate to local conditions.
	Acceptability of combined credit/extension package to small farmers undetermined.	3. Testing of farm records system, including level of participation by farmers.	3. Identifies critical categories of data and uses in decisionmaking by both farmers and paratechnicians.

components identified in the final PPs.

The matrix shows several threads running through this set of projects, all addressing the same general problem -- raising productivity and income in a population of small farmers -- from similar perspectives. They emphasize the need for testing in order to identify appropriate technologies, rather than specifying technological choices *a priori.*

Equally in evidence is the inclusion of an information system as an integral project component in each of the designs. The information system is not intended to be an independent component, because it forms the basis for decisionmaking across all project components; it generates criteria for measuring results wherever specific tests are being carried out. To cite one example, in the Tanzania Farmer Training Project the information system (Component 5) will monitor the tests of production technologies (Component 2), evaluate their results and identify problems that require further testing.

Because in each instance the situations and content, even of the information system, are considered subject to modification, the designs fall far short of prescribing clearly defined "experimental" procedures. From the matrix in Figure 7.2, the reader cannot easily visualize how the various tests are to be conducted. Yet failure to observe the strictness of classical social experimentation is deliberate and represents an explicit choice in the projects' designs. The fact that certain critics have dwelt on this point suggests a need for further clarification of some conceptual and operational issues raised by the process approach. This will be followed by a presentation of guidelines for designing actual tests.

SOME BROADER CONSIDERATIONS

Conceptual Issues

Most development projects operate in situations that reduce, if they do not actually eliminate, the possibility of conducting social experimentation as it is usually conceived. The following definition encompasses the principal features of classical social experimentation:

> By experiment is meant that one or more treatments (programs) are administered to some set of persons (or other units) drawn

> at *random* from a specified population; and that observations (or *measurements*) are made to learn how (or *how much*) some relevant aspect of their behavior following treatment differs from like behavior on the part of an untreated or control group also drawn at random from the same population.[1]

The function of social experimentation is to provide knowledge for decisions about how to intervene in areas of social policy. In this respect the questions posed are similar to those confronting the staff of a small farmer development project. Critical differences arise, however, in the degree of control that development practitioners are actually able to exercise, at reasonable cost, over the environment they work in. The selection of field-testing sites in a project context comes about only through interaction between development practitioners and other interested parties (including host country authorities, donor agency officials, and -- at least in theory -- members of the prospective target population). These critical real-world variables force the prospective social "experimenter" to tailor his strategy to specific circumstances.

The usual outcome of this process is a decrease in the control available to the "experimenter." In a field context, randomization, which ensures equivalence between the group(s) subjected to "treatment"(s) and an untreated control group, is a difficult procedure (sometimes impossible) and generally a costly one.[2] As a second-best solution one may adopt "quasi-experimental" techniques, which seek to match treated and untreated groups across as many relevant variables as possible. The rigor of these techniques determines the level of explanatory power (interpretability) in the results of the tests.

From this perspective it appears that certain of the testing activities incorporated in the twelve projects constitute potential "quasi-experiments." To achieve this potential, however, they require more detailed elaboration in the form of carefully structured plans for executing the tests, each of which should be framed in such a way as to examine a particular hypothesis.[3] Relatively few hypotheses have been stated explicitly in the projects' documentation: An intuitive, empirical approach is indicated, with the expectation that hypotheses will be formulated, tested, refined, retested, and so on as implementation proceeds. This open-ended quality may represent the optimal response to the uncertainties encountered in the design phase. It means, though, that reference to "experimentation" in the documentation is colloquial rather than technical, since no true "experimental" designs have been generated in the Project Papers.

It also seems probable that activities in the areas of greatest uncertainty will have to depend on something less than even "second best": they may not attain the level of "quasi-experiments," either for lack of definitive hypotheses, or due to an inability to identify and control for all the variables potentially influencing the problems under investigation. This should not be taken to mean, however, that such tests will fail to produce useful results. Given the urgency of the problems confronting small farmers in many of these project situations, identification of techniques that work may justify full-scale application even if the reasons that they do are not fully understood. For example, a great deal can be learned in a *post hoc* analysis of a "treated" population by investigating why some small farmers adopted a particular intervention and others did not.

In another critical respect, the testing procedures envisioned in the twelve projects studied differ from classical social experimentation. Testing of a particular alternative is not pursued indefinitely, but only as long as it appears promising. For example, tests during a single crop season of four to six months may yield enough evidence to justify dropping an agricultural input from the inventory of possible interventions. More complex tests -- for example, comparing the results of reliance on alternative methods of knowledge transfer between farmers -- would require continuous monitoring over longer periods (perhaps the full life of this project). Depending on the focus of a project component, adaptive research may begin with a larger number of possible techniques, but the range will be progressively narrowed. So long as this process is purposive and systematic, it is logical to expect finally to identify optimal techniques for the project to introduce in the target area.

Time and Resource Constraints

During its involvement with project design, DAI encountered considerable resistance to the notion of evolutionary project development. This resistance took two principal forms: in certain quarters the "unknowns" were perceived as much less serious constraints to successful implementation than DAI claimed; the argument was also made that there was "no time" for adaptive research. These two positions are in fact mutually reinforcing, and in Niger and Haiti they eventually carried the day.

These objections can be countered on a general level by drawing on the *Strategies* report[4] for evidence of the difficulties involved in mobilizing local involvement in small farmer development projects. On a country-specific level too, it is usually possible, without having to range too far, to document the limitations of conventional "packaged" approaches, if indeed any have been mounted in the small farm sector. The scarcity of proven answers, and the logic of adaptive research in developing them, would seem to offer ample justification for trying out the process approach in actual field settings.

Even so, when it comes to the task of assembling a project on the ground, the "no need" and "no time" objections must be reckoned with. They are an interesting manifestation of what one American commentator has referred to as "Timpane's Law," paraphrased as follows:

> If there is enough interest and concern in the country and in the Congress to support an experiment about a particular problem, that interest and concern will be so great that people will not be willing to wait long enough for an experiment to be carried out before enacting legislation and launching programs. On the other hand, if there is not that extraordinary degree of interest in the problem, then there won't be enough interest to support an experiment. So either way there is no experiment.[5]

One has only to substitute "AID and host country government" for "the country and the Congress," and "committing funds" for "enacting legislation," to recognize that this formulation applies to the problems encountered in project design. Its internal logic resembles Catch-22, for either (1) adequate time is available but the required resources are not forthcoming; or (2) the decision to commit resources indicates a level of urgency and a demand for instant results that foreshorten the time allotted to do the testing.

These are the considerations that impinge most directly on the elaboration of a project framework. They virtually guarantee that, whatever rhetorical commitments are made to "experimentation," the actual testing procedures carried out within the project will tend to be much less sophisticated, and less powerful in terms of their explanatory content, than the standard procedures on which classical social experimentation is based.

There are important trade-offs in this area. What is sacrificed in the way of sophisticated design may be more than compensated for by the creation of an indigenous capacity to continue exploratory testing and adaptive research after the conclusion of the project. Local human resources are frequently not well matched with the requirements of a full-blown "experimental" design. One response to this difficulty would involve recruiting large numbers of social scientists, with the aim of ensuring rigorous adherence to scientific procedures and irrefutable, unambiguous results from the tests being conducted. A second response, which is demonstrably more sensible in both the short and long terms, is to tailor the requirements of the testing procedures to the local situation. In other words, the technical assistance team should enhance the ability of key actors in the project area (local officials, technicians and extension staff, and farmers themselves) to conceptualize, structure, and execute the tests. The primary function of the tests is to generate criteria for decisionmaking, and this responsibility must ultimately devolve on local actors.

In the twelve projects, concerted efforts were made to build in situationally appropriate agendas for adaptive research. In Chile and Colombia, for example, both the information system and the content of other components take cognizance of existing personnel resources and comparatively high literacy rates among the target population of small farmers. By comparison, the suggested procedures for the Ethiopia project are elementary in nature, but include anticipated increases in sophistication as the method becomes institutionalized.

Ethical Issues

The ethical implications of testing in field settings overlap partially with the practical issues discussed in the previous section. While ethical issues have not always received their due in social experimentation, the nature of the process approach exercises certain controls on the conduct of field tests. The emphasis on collaboration and involvement of local actors (farmers, paratechnicians, local leadership, etc.) helps to ensure that the selection of "treatments" and their allocation to groups are acceptable in the immediate project environment. The evaluation of results, furthermore, is meant to be part and parcel of a locally based decisionmaking process.

Although these features of the process approach offer important safeguards against abuses in the implementation of field-testing, they cannot guarantee absolute protection of the human subjects affected by the tests. To make sure that the main problem areas and associated danger signals are not lost to sight, they are briefly summarized below.[6]

Privacy

There are two principal dimensions to this issue where field-testing is concerned. The first involves the strategy and techniques of observation, since "unobtrusive" research is usually unsuited to the kinds of tests being run in rural development projects. The duration and frequency of visits by persons charged with collecting information, the nature of the information being sought, and the personal interaction between suppliers and recorders of information are all potential sources of irritation and even noncooperation. Given the nature of the projects as designed, noncooperation can serve as the small farmer's "ultimate weapon" if the nuisance value of continual observations outweighs the prospective benefits to be drawn from the test.

The second dimension of privacy concerns the handling of information after it has been collected. Coding and storage procedures may have to take account of individual's vulnerability to harassment or exploitation. While it would seem on the surface that the sort of information sought in a small farmer development project would be of little interest to anyone but farmers and project staff, this cannot automatically be assumed. The clearest example of awareness of this problem is in the documentation for the Zaire project, where project designers had to consider methods for shielding economic data on individual farmers from agents (traditional *agronomes*) with a reputation for arbitrary and illegal taxing and confiscation of property.

Exposure to Risks

The introduction of interventions into an agricultural production system carries along the risk of unsatisfactory results, portending economic hardship or even disaster for the test participants. Risk-sharing, as described in detail in several of the Project Papers (e.g., Colombia, Chile, Zaire), represents an attempt to combat this difficulty by anticipating the small farmer's perception of risks. In essence, risk-sharing schemes are meant to elicit participation in field tests of new technologies, by guaranteeing small farmers a minimum income (given a reasonable outlay of effort) in the event that the technologies fail.

Exposure to political risks is an implicit rather than explicit issue in the twelve projects discussed in this report. By definition, however, "decisionmaking" refers to a political process in which scarce resources are allocated. Seeking to alter that process by strengthening its participatory content, as several of the designs imply, opens up potentially serious questions. In Afghanistan, for example, the prospect of changing the distribution of water among small farmers poses a threat to the leadership that currently decide who gets how much water. Although the projects are not intended as vehicles for political interference, it should be recognized that development can never be completely divorced from political processes.

In this context it is important to anticipate the potential response of various interest groups to activities undertaken by the project. During implementation two elements appear especially significant for protecting the interests of project participants against sanctions available to entrenched local interest groups. The first is the confidentiality of information gathering and processing techniques; the second is the visible demonstration of the host country government's commitment to the goals and activities of the project.

Manipulation of Subjects

Criticism of testing procedures, on the ground that they deliberately withhold "treatments" from one segment of the population, can be countered in the light of the preceding discussion of time and resource constraints. In the first place, testing is not advocated as an end in itself, and interventions found unsuitable are eliminated from the inventory of possible techniques. In the second place, the interweaving of adaptive research, field-testing, and application (benefit distribution) is such that the length of the "withholding" period will be kept to a minimum.

A further safeguard against manipulation is the voluntary nature of participation in the tests. In other words, for many of the farm-level tests (involving adoption of new techniques such as chemical fertilizers), individual farmers will not be forced to join the "treatment" group if they do not wish to do so; and if the intervention is a surefire success, those who were in the "control" group in the first year of the trials can be rapidly assimilated into the "treatment" group in the second year and thereafter.

SOME GUIDELINES FOR DESIGNING FIELD TESTS

Most field tests in projects based on the process approach, it has been argued, will represent second-best or third-best use of "experimental" procedures. They will be quasi-experimental" (using nonrandom assignment of subjects), or, failing that, they will rely on intuitive comparisons between generally similar populations. It becomes necessary, then, to take a closer look at these less-than-optimal designs, focusing on three major questions:

- Analytical control over the environment: How does the designer of a field test establish a modicum of control over definition and choice of the target population in order to be able to interpret the results? What constitutes a manageable set of variables on which to base comparisons of treated and untreated groups?
- Techniques that provide the best access to the population: In many of the twelve project settings the question of how to intervene (through which formal and informal local institutions) was left subject to testing during the implementation phase.
- Once access has been established, the actual content of appropriate interventions must be worked out empirically by analyzing the results of field trials. This is the key to the entire exercise, but the explanations provided in the documentation for the twelve projects are abstract; they do not give a clear picture of how tests would be run or how the results relate to decisionmaking.

The remainder of this chapter examines these three issues with reference to concrete examples.

Analytical Control

To approach this question we shall begin with a hypothetical situation and then examine one case from among the twelve projects. It will become apparent that the procedure is reductionist and tends to oversimplify the realities of the project environment. The complexity of the problems being addressed and the nature of proposed interventions will determine whether those realities have been distorted to an excessive degree.

In the hypothetical case, we start with the assumption that the project environment contains four critical variables distinguishing members of the target population of small farmers. There are two values for each variable, and coding may be performed in the following fashion:

- Ecological zone: Codes E_1, E_2;
- Farm size: Codes S_1, S_2;
- Technology level: Codes T_1, T_2; and
- Crop mix: Codes C_1, C_2.

This coding system generates $2^4 = 16$ possible combinations. Carving the target population into 16 matched groups, however, will frequently be too time-consuming and costly.

It is possible, with the use of rapid survey techniques, to establish the general distribution of these variants. Let us suppose that a survey is carried out, and it is found that five combinations account for ± 90 percent of the total. This would provide a basis for constructing a set of only five matched groups. It might also be found, as a result of a rapid survey, that the amount of variance within a particular feature being investigated is so low that it justifies dropping that variable from the set. In this way, too, analytical control over the environment can be strengthened. Rapid surveys also help to isolate the most disadvantaged group or groups of farmers: The $E_2S_2T_1C_2$ variant, for example, with the "problem areas" being continued dependence on an unproductive technology, T_1, and a crop mix, C_2, that offers little potential for increased income.

This procedure, in its broad outlines, can be applied in any project environment. The critical point of departure is agreement on the minimal set of variables, and from there on the minimal set of values attached to them. (Note that in theory only two variables might be designated as critical for a given target population, but a much larger number of values might have to be accommodated in the definition of groups for interventions and control.)

Among the set of twelve projects studied, the Upper Volta Women's Project illustrates how broad cuts on variations within the project environment help to define the field setting for testing activities. The design team focused on two variables: the presence or absence of year-round access to water in each village, and the existence of a dependable cash crop. (Clearly these variables were linked, since the existence of income-generating cash crops proved to be a function of water availability.) This breakdown generated a classification of three "levels" of village development: Level One referred to those villages lacking both year-round water _and_ a cash crop; Level Two designated those with water but without a cash crop, and Level Three encompassed those villages possessing both characteristics.

This three-tiered classification provided a useful starting point in comparing performance across villages in different project activities. A principal component of the Upper Volta Women's Project was a fund for promoting small enterprise development in the villages. This simple method of "carving up" the project environment was appropriate for the type of comparative analysis needed during project implementation. One form of analysis would involve measuring the impact of similar interventions (e.g., grain milling enterprises owned and operated by women's groups) in Level One, Two and Three villages. A second form of analysis would entail measuring the impact of interventions tailored to a particular category (e.g., Level Two villages), with a number of villages in this category being "treated" and others serving as "controls."

Establishing Access

The Afghanistan Integrated Rural Development Project, among others, was conceived in an environment characterized by more numerous and complex "unknowns" than in Upper Volta. In the view of the DAI design team, this situation provided ample justification for an avowedly "experimental" approach to project development.[7] Although the AID Mission and the host country government desired a district-level project, there was no sound basis for designating one district rather than another as "representative" of Afghan conditions. Substantial diversity was known to exist among ecological zones, agricultural and livestock systems, sociocultural groupings and local-level political institutions, and in the absence of meaningful parameters for these variations, no "modal" district could be identified.

The design team worked under the premise that, in such fluid and undefined circumstances, meaningful understanding of how to intervene could best be developed from the bottom up. Most of the intervention activities suggested in the design paper would have specific impact in small group settings and would be unlikely to have immediate spread effects. It was argued that, if control could be established in small group settings and meaningful results obtained from initial testing procedures, more generalizable lessons would emerge as the project progressed.

To illustrate how the approach was intended to operate within the Mohammad Agha District, we may examine the Technology and Agricultural Production component. In the field report, three areas of activity were identified: Availability of Water, Distribution of Water, and On-Farm Water Use. Figure 7.3 shows how the project environment might be "carved up" (at different levels of precision) to set the stage for systematic testing in each area. The units listed on the matrix were not mentioned explicitly in the design paper; they represent implicit distinctions based on the design team's limited exposure to the project environment and their attempt to amass survey data during that time.

These procedures provide a point of departure for a difficult exercise: determining how to intervene effectively over time. The project was conceived as a framework within which the process could be begun. Interventions could be tried, organizations formed, services provided, and eventually, new behavior patterns among the small farmer population could be established.

The difficulty of the exercise lies in the lack of a proven strategy for entering the local communi-

FIGURE 7.3

TECHNOLOGY AND AGRICULTURAL PRODUCTION COMPONENT
AFGHANISTAN INTEGRATED RURAL DEVELOPMENT PROJECT

Focus of Activity	Possible Units of Analysis	Analytical Procedures
Availability of Water	• Irrigation System canal = S_1 karez = S_2 • Location along system near origin = L_1 midpoint = L_2 endpoint = L_3	Distinguish between water availability constraints in two systems. Select target areas (localities) of each type for testing activities. Determine water availability at various points along the distribution system.
Distribution of Water	• Irrigation System S_1, S_2 • Location L_1, L_2, L_3 • Local group's decisionmaking authoritarian = D_1 consensual = D_2	Construct sample of local groups in each system: S_1, S_2 Through monitoring of decisionmaking on water allocation, analytically distinguish D_1 from D_2 groups. Identify constraints on equitable distribution, distinguishing between S_1D_1 and S_2D_1 groups.
On-Farm Water Use	• Irrigation System S_1, S_2 • Location L_1, L_2, L_3 • Local Groups D_1, D_2 • Types of Users: Landowners = U_1 Sharecroppers = U_2 Pastoralists = U_3	Construct sample for each irrigation system, comprising proportionate numbers of users (U_1, U_2, U_3) at each location. Distinguish water needs and usage among U_1, U_2, U_3. Isolate best technology (management of scarce water) being practiced. Determine potential for transfer of technology within D_1, D_2 groups, at locations L_1, L_2, L_3.

ties. The possibilities are as follows (paired options representing poles of a continuum):

- Entry through officially designated leadership; or entry through groups of farmers with a common interest (e.g., apple growers, grape growers).

- Entry by professionals representing the government; or entry by paraprofessionals from the local communities.

- Entry through established local officials currently working at the district level; or entry through a new group of officials not previously associated with the area.

- Entry through women and women's groups; or entry through male heads-of-household.

- Entry through progressive large landholders; or entry through the acknowledged poor and underprivileged.

Midpoints in these continua provide still more options, without even touching upon questions of technology, of the relationship between social services (health) and productive services (water),or of the formal mechanisms for generating local institutions and interest groups. This exercise provides a framework for applying different intervention methods. A project must proceed from application (a successful entry into a village) to the next step (a useful technological suggestion to be applied) in an ordered sequence. The method of approach, the ordering of the sequences, and the methodology of the applications, are the critical elements in this stage of the project. A technical understanding of agricultural production possibilities can then be applied in subsequent stages.

Content of Interventions

Once appropriate units of measurement have been identified in the project environment, and access to the target population has been achieved, the specific content of interventions must be worked out. The twelve project designs usually stopped short of specifying priorities or providing an itemized breakdown of the proposed testing program. Subsequent

DAI experience with planning for and practicing project implementation has sharpened our understanding of how such a program would operate in an actual field situation.

Agricultural field-testing and "quasi-experimentation" proposed for the Ghana DIPRUD project provide a useful illustration. Figure 7.4 presents a simplified agricultural calendar for Atebubu District, the site of this project. The major responsibilities of the project's Agricultural Advisor during the first year (pre-implementation phase) are shown at the bottom of the figure. Distinct ecological zones and associated cropping patterns must be delineated prior to the intensive field surveys.

The initial surveys would identify the cropping cycles and complex cropping patterns that exist within the project environment and focus on farmer attitudes towards production constraints, specifically on perceptions of the following types of risk:

- The risk of crop failure due to natural catastrophe;

- The risk of crop failure due to reliance on unproven or improperly used technologies;

- The risk of post-harvest failure due to an inability to market farm produce; and

- The risk of debt due to poor market prices, or production levels insufficient to meet the cost of credit.

Three to four months would be considered a minimum amount of time to devote to observation before specifying interventions in an agricultural environment where "smallholders have developed over generations, a complex cropping pattern which is efficient given the ecological setting, the prevailing level of technology and the land and labor resources under their command." [8]

The surveys will serve two important functions. First they will provide a basis for designing field trials of possible innovations on small farmers' own land, utilizing risk-sharing agreements between farmers and project management. Second, the surveys will delineate the optimal structure and content of a farm records subsystem within the overall information system created by the project.

FIGURE 7.4

SIMPLIFIED AGRICULTURAL CALENDAR, PRE-IMPLEMENTATION PHASE: ATEBUBU DISTRICT DEVELOPMENT PROJECT (GHANA)

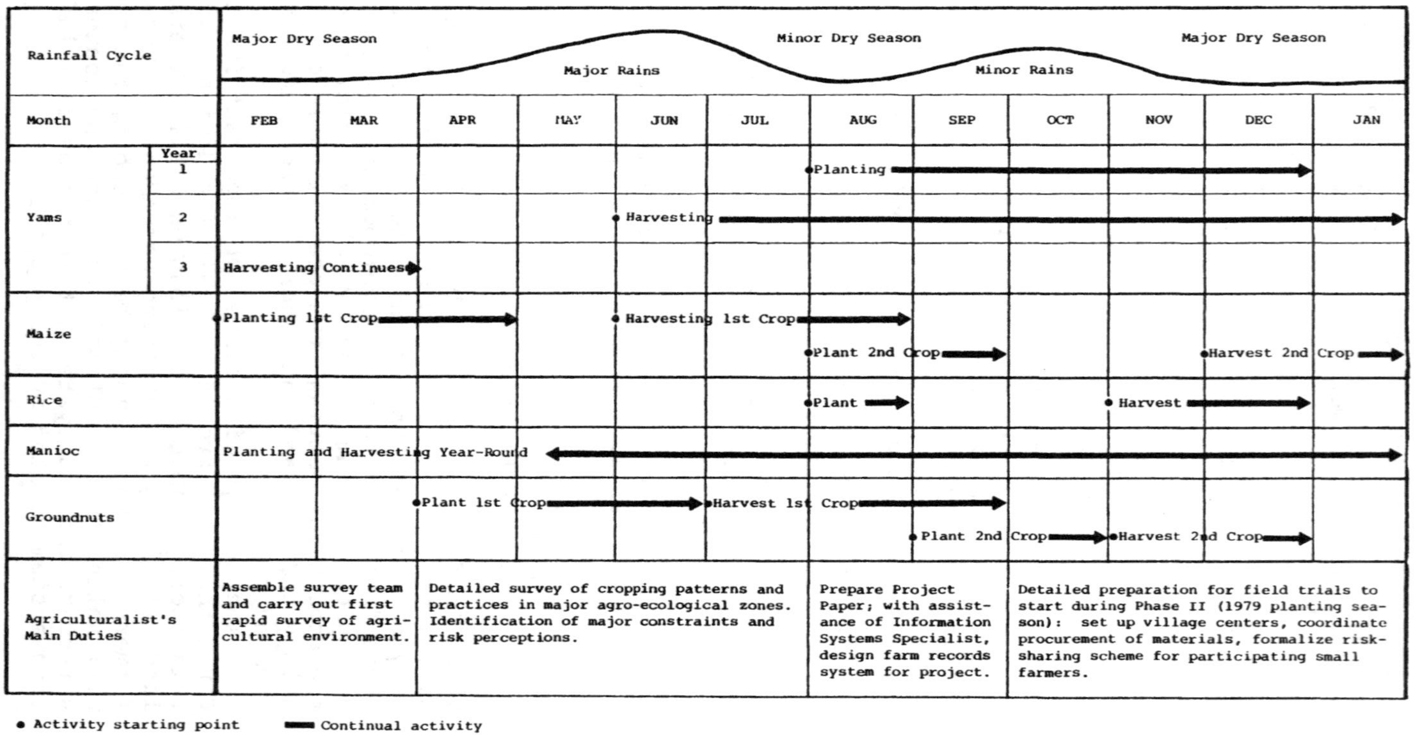

A fully elaborated testing program would be introduced prior to the start of the planting season in the second year of the project. To establish priorities in this program, detailed survey results would be needed, but the general orientation of the DIPRUD project provides some basic guidelines:

- Avoidance of early dependence on imported materials, consultants, etc., and the associated problems of foreign exchange requirements, lead time for delivery of materials, and availability of exotic inputs;
- Full evaluation and utilization of local human and material resources; and
- Potential replicability, taking into account available resources in other districts, as well as Atebubu itself.

When these criteria are applied to what is currently known about the farming systems of the district, distinctions can be drawn between three approaches to improving agricultural production. From this it is possible to establish a tentative ranking of the three in terms of their priority. The ranking, as well as the examples on the following list, would be subject to modification when a better picture is obtained from initial surveys and the project's information system.

Priority I:

Identification and testing of apparently successful practices and technologies already being used by the most progressive small farmers in the area, and which can be spread to other farmers, using basic extension methods and locally available materials. Examples might include:

A. Cultivar Selection

1. Local high yielding varieties
2. Fertilizer responsive varieties
3. Desirable growth forms
4. Longer storage life varieties

B. Farm Practices

1. Seedbed preparation
2. Manuring and fertilization
3. Cultural techniques

Priority II:

Identification and testing of modified local practices and technologies requiring outside input from Ghanaian research organizations and with low to moderate foreign exchange requirements. Examples might include:

A. Improved cultivars from formal breeding programs

B. Modified land management patterns

1. Intercropping of legume/nonlegume crops
2. Tree crops
3. Monoculture trials
4. Fallow land regeneration under harvestable plants, e.g., legume-grass mixes for pasture and/or fodder production

C. Animal traction

Priority III:

Identification and testing of new practices or technologies requiring greater capital investment and/or foreign exchange, imported expertise, and longer lead times necessary for experimentation and evaluation before implementation. These might include:

A. High yielding varieties (HYVs) and associated input packages (Note: Need to determine HYV compatibility with intercropping systems, e.g., critical timing of interplanting so that yields of HYV and associated crop are not lowered.)

B. Fertilizer trials

1. Seedbed incorporation
2. Side dressing
3. Foliar applications

C. Tractorization and management of tractorization

1. Walking, wheel, and track types
2. Gasoline and/or diesel
3. Use trials
4. Auxiliary uses

For purposes of illustration, let us assume that initial surveys confirm the ranking of priorities, and that a decision is made to focus on the problem of yam decay. Post-harvest losses in this crop have already been identified as a serious constraint, limiting the ability of farmers to market the crop successfully. Optimum storage conditions (both refrigerated and non-refrigerated) have been identified in scientific journals.[9] Non-refrigerated yam storage life has been estimated at three to four months. Yet there is wide variation in loss figures due to cultivar differences, varying physical damage during harvest, handling and transportation, and depredations of rodents, insects and disease. The picture is further complicated by the fact that three different species of yam are grown in Ghana, and often in the same field by an individual farmer.

We will assume, too, that the survey work has generated the two following hypotheses:

- That cultivar "A" (not widely grown in the district) is substantially more resistant to decay than cultivar "B," which was found to be the most commonly grown variety of yam; or

- That a low-cost storage technique "X" (not currently in use on most Atebubu District farms) offers greater protection than "Y," which is the most commonly practiced method for storing yams.

A simple "quasi-experiment" can then be designed to determine the impact of interventions "A" and "X," whether introduced separately or in combination. It requires the designation of four groups of farmers.

- The A-X group will grow the new variety of yam and store it using new recommended techniques;

- The A-Y group will grow the new variety of yam and store it using traditional techniques;

- The B-X group will grow the traditional variety of yam and store it using recommended new techniques; and

- The B-Y group will serve as a control, growing the traditional variety and using traditional storage methods.

The following guidelines will help to ensure meaningful and interpretable results: the groups should be of comparable size (a minimum of 15 to 20 farmers in each seems desirable), and matched for a minimal set of key environmental variables. While the latter cannot be specified in advance of careful survey work, it is probable that the size of the area under cultivation, ecological zone, and availability of manual labor in the farmer's household would need to be included.

The turnaround time in obtaining results will necessarily vary according to the type of agricultural activity. If the test described here were begun with the yam planting season of August/September 1978, meaningful results would not be obtained until the end of 1979 or beginning of 1980, when yam harvesting had been completed and a storage period of several months had elapsed (see Figure 7.4).

On the other hand, comparable tests affecting groundnut or maize production would yield results within a span of four to five months. It would become possible to disseminate successful techniques to other farmers at a much earlier date, perhaps with the second planting season in 1979 or the first one in 1980. Determination of effective extension techniques (to ensure rapid spead of knowledge acquired in the field trials) will require a comparable level of effort and willingness to test various approaches. Thus the technical field trials are not an end in themselves; they must be integrated with the other components of the project.

CONCLUSIONS

The purpose of this chapter was to examine the provisions for "experimentation" in the twelve projects under review and to determine what general lessons could be drawn about the operational meaning of the term in rural development projects. It was found that the actual environments in which projects must operate place severe constraints on the feasibility of "experimentation," as it is conventionally construed. Indeed, the characterization of the twelve projects as "experiments" appeared in retrospect to have been evocative, but technically incorrect.

The analysis showed that, aside from being costly and difficult to effect, classical "experimental" procedures are not the optimal basis for the type of learning process that the projects seek to promote. The optimal procedures, while second- or third-best from a scientific viewpoint, have a sound pragmatic orientation. They involve imaginative use of field tests and continuing adaptive research, with direct involvement of local actors. A two-way information flow was built into each of the DAI project designs to ensure that, as answers to specific problems are worked out, they are fed back into the planning and design process. The explanatory power of results will tend to vary, and the level of abstraction in those results will tend to be lower than if more rigorous "experiments" had been mounted (at substantially greater cost and consuming longer periods of time) by observers with an academic orientation.

In sum, a strong case can be made for the conduct of adaptive research and the testing of prospective interventions in field settings. These activities form an integral part of the process approach to project development, and they are the vehicles that make it possible for an incremental learning process to proceed.

NOTES

1 Henry W. Riecken and Robert F. Boruch, eds., *Social Experimentation: A Method for Planning and Evaluating Social Intervention*, New York: Academic Press, 1974.

2 Randomization permits the analyst of experimental results to conclude that the treatment alone accounts for observed differences between treated and untreated populations. For an extensive discussion of experimental design, see Thomas D. Cook and Donald T. Campbell, "The Design and Conduct of Quasi-Experiments and True Experiments in Field Settings," in *Handbook of Industrial and Organizational Psychology,* Marvin D. Dunnette, ed., New York: Rand McNally, 1976, pp. 223-326; and Riecken and Boruch, op. cit.

3 It is worth remarking here that a useful rule of thumb in constructing an hypothesis is that it must be capable of being proved incorrect. Hence the more specific and limited the hypothesis (e.g., A is associated with B), the more easily it can be tested. Conversely, inclusive "catch-all" statements (e.g., A, B, C, D, and E contribute to phenomenon F) are more difficult to disprove, and generally require multivariate analysis.

4 E. R. Morss, J. K. Hatch, D. R. Mickelwait, and C. F. Sweet, *Strategies for Small Farmer Development* (two volumes), Boulder, Colo.: Westview Press, 1976.

5 M. Timpane, "Educational Experimentation in National Social Policy," *Harvard Educational Review,* 40:547-566, 1970, cited and paraphrased by John W. Evans in "Motives for Experimentation," in *Proceedings of Conference on Social Experiments*, August 1974,

National Science Foundation, Science and Technology Policy Office, March 9, 1975.

[6] For a more complete discussion of ethical problems in experimentation, see Chapter 8 of Riecken and Boruch, op. cit.

[7] In retrospect, and in line with the preceding discussion, the use of the term "experiment" appears to have been more colloquial than technical. Better understanding of the issues and use of a less ambitious terminology might have spared the project some of the challenges and delays it has endured since the submission of the design team's field report. See Chapter 3.

[8] *Ghana Agricultural Sector Assessment*, USAID/Accra, December 1974, p. 50.

[9] See, for example, O. M. Adeniji, "Influence of Moisture and Temperature on Yam Decay Organisms," in *Phytopathology* 60: 698-99, 1970.

8
Reflections on Project Organization and Implementation

Implementation is a neglected issue in development. In AID, as well as in other development organizations, most of the rewards (attracting most of the brains) flow from project development rather than project implementation. Few direct-hire AID employees have served as managers of technical assistance teams although those serving overseas often have oversight responsibility for such teams. It is rare, moreover, for those AID employees who help design a project to later have any direct responsibility for implementing it.

Yet early attention to organizational and implementation arrangements is exceedingly important. It is necessary to determine who will do what for whom, when and how. This means working with the host country to select the implementation agency, identify senior personnel, generate a budget, staff, vehicles, transportation, housing, and the like. Tackling the details of staffing, funding and control linkages is too often put off or handled through the Conditions Precedent requirement that an appropriate implementation plan be prepared by the implementing agency prior to disbursement of funds. However, this process tends to exclude the PP designers, who may have the best knowledge of how the project might work, from having assisted in the details of implementation planning and the organizational aspects of project management.

A central proposition of this chapter is that careful attention to organizational arrangements at the time of design can keep problems encountered during implementation to a minimum. In particular, three issues involving implementation/organizational arrangements deserve careful consideration during design exercises:

- Project management strategies;
- Building flexibility and redesign capacity into project management; and
- Project decisionmaking structure.

Drawing on DAI rural development design and evaluation experience over the last two years, this chapter will discuss some of the problems commonly encountered in project implementation that can be anticipated and dealt with during project design.[1]

PROJECT MANAGEMENT STRATEGIES

Arriving at optimal management arrangements for project implementation, including the selection of a principal implementing entity, requires an understanding of the objectives, activities and resource requirements of the project and an in-depth knowledge of the host country's political, administrative and organizational dynamics. The choices available within the context of a given project and a given country are generally small in number. The practical constraints of working with existing organizations, existing personnel and existing capabilities frequently require thinking in terms of second- or third-best solutions, rather than theoretically desirable arrangements.

DAI's experience over the past several years indicates that there are four recurring types of management strategies commonly designed into or adopted by rural development projects:

- Working through traditional line ministries, or agencies affiliated with line ministries, at the national level;
- Working through subnational governments or government agencies;
- Working through integrated development agencies; and
- Creating special project management units.

The use of these arrangements in actual project situations, together with the advantages and disadvantages of such arrangements, are discussed in this section.

Working Through Traditional Line Ministries

In four of the projects -- Chile, Haiti, Colombia, and Tanzania - FT -- the management strategy adopted was to locate project management responsibility in a traditional line ministry. In all four cases this was either the Ministry of Agriculture or an agency under or affiliated with the Ministry of Agriculture. There were several reasons, some theoretical and others practical, for selecting this management strategy for these four projects. First, the ministry or agency is a permanent part of the government. Knowledge gained and new ideas and approaches tried and found successful in the project might, therefore, spread to other programs run by the same agency. Second, the best goal of the four projects was an increase in the income and productivity of small farmers, so it made sense to lean toward the national-level agency with the agricultural sector charter. Third, none of the four projects was limited to a specific area of the country, so it was not possible to work through a local organization or a subnational government entity. In at least two cases, Colombia and Tanzania - FT, the project had been _requested_ by the organization that became its manager, thus effectively narrowing the choice of implementation organizations down to one.[2]

Working through traditional line ministries also has a number of disadvantages. The principal disadvantage is that the capabilities of line ministries are generally limited to one or two narrowly defined functional areas, while rural development projects increasingly require the integration of a variety of functional activities. In order to carry out this variety of activities, the designated agency often must look to outside sources of expertise and capability. Another problem is that traditional ministries usually have their most capable personnel in the capital city, with much weaker capabilities in the rural areas where project activities will actually be conducted. In addition, ministries or large national agencies have many different programs, so that there is sometimes a problem of how much priority and attention the project will receive within the ministry or agency itself. Another problem is that, when operational responsibility for project activities is delegated to a particular office within a ministry, that office sometimes had difficulty securing the cooperation of other offices within the same ministry.

Thus, in the four projects where the traditional line ministry approach was adopted, it became necessary to see how the agency could forge links to external organizations whose cooperation would be necessary, as well as how it might organize to coordinate its own internal activities and allocate operational responsibilities between headquarters and the field. This required different tactics in each project, mainly because the concept of what constituted the field differed dramatically among the four. In Chile, the field consisted of private sector cooperatives through which the project would be implemented in its initial stages. The government's role is to set policy, make subsidy payments for several years, and monitor and evaluate the performance of private sector technical assistance. Only a country with strong local institutions and a well-developed and highly skilled inventory of human resources in the private agricultural sector could work through such organizational arrangements.

In the Haiti project, the field is a geographic area. The design, unfortunately, contains little specification of how national-level and field-level interaction should take place. The design does call for an expatriate team of management/administration specialists to set up a special project implementation unit within the Ministry of Agriculture (a ministry with responsibilities ranging from extension and price controls to conservation and running rural schools), but is not clear about how this team should function within the ministry.

In the Colombia project, the design called for implementation by the national-level Agriculture and Livestock Institute (ICA), working through three regional offices. Although ICA is a highly experienced organization with capable personnel, it became apparent during project design that the Institute would need help with the integration of its activities to support new approaches to rural development, as well as help with the monitoring and evaluation unit of the project. Special units and technical assistance were designed into the project to overcome these problems. But one year into implementation of the Colombia Small Farmer Development Project, neither special units nor technical assistance existed.

Similar assignments and balance between national- and field-level involvement exist in the Tanzania Farmer Training Project. This project also called for technical assistance and for new mechanisms -- Farmer Training Wings and Mobile Farm Assistance

Units -- to be established within the Ministry of Agriculture Training Units (MATIs), which were tapped as the implementing agencies for the project.

Working Through Subnational Government Entities

The increasing popularity of integrated or area development projects coordinated among development agencies has coincided in many countries with a movement toward decentralization -- the devolution of decisionmaking authority and the control of development resources, from the center toward the periphery of government. At the same time, it has been increasingly recognized that the best project implementation results can be achieved by locating primary operational responsibility at the lowest capable administrative level.[3]

One problem with this principle is that, the lower one looks on the administrative scale, the lower, in all likelihood, are the government's administrative capabilities. The talent gap in developing countries typically finds an urban-rural, center-periphery expression:

> The best brains, the 'best people' are concentrated in the capital city, and this centralization feeds upon itself, attacting the best of each new crop of young men to it. Career-opportunity, intellectual company, social life, all pull against the prospect of work in a distant province.[4]

The problem is compounded by the fact that most developing countries have made very little effort to create viable rural institutions with which decentralized authorities can work.

There are exceptions. Several countries where DAI helped design projects have taken positive steps toward decentralization and assignment of authority to lower levels.[5] As a consequence it became possible in these countries to situate project management responsibility at some subnational level. Table 8.1 evaluates the status of effective decentralization in the ten countries where DAI helped design projects, and shows the implementation arrangements that were eventually selected for each project.

TABLE 8.1

DECENTRALIZATION AND THE CHOICE OF IMPLEMENTATION ARRANGEMENTS

Project	Project is Area-Specific	Effective Decentralization[1]	Location of Primary Implementation Organization
Tanzania - VD	Yes	5	Regional and District Governments
Tanzania - FT	No	5	National Agency Working through local branches with Agency
Ethiopia	Yes	4	Provincial Government
Upper Volta - OP	No	4	A semiautonomous national development agency
Upper Volta - WP	Yes	4	Regional development organizations
Ghana	Yes	3	District Councils
Niger	Yes	3	Regional and Arrondissement Development Committees supervised by a national agency
Colombia	No	2	National agency working through branch agencies
Zaire	Yes	2	Independent Project Management Unit
Haiti	Yes	1	National ministry working through locally based personnel
Afghanistan	Yes	1	National development agency working with local line ministry offices
Chile	No	1	National Commission and a Private Cooperative Board

[1] Scale: 1 (low) to 5 (high). This scale represents a judgment concerning the extent to which each of the ten project countries has devolved effective development decisonmaking authority to subnational units of government.

The Case of Tanzania

The most effective devolution has occurred in Tanzania where, at every level of the political/administrative structure, primary development authority is vested in an officer representing the Prime Minister's Office. Although local line ministry staff receive support from their national offices and retain responsibilities for carrying out a variety of functional programs at the local level, it is to the Prime Minister's representative that they are responsible. This officer is charged with planning and carrying out development activities and receives a funding grant from the national government to implement the plan, with substantial freedom to allocate and reallocate these funds as needed. The key to the development officer's effectiveness is the power to hire, fire, and promote technical personnel.

It was in this structural context, at the regional and district levels, that the Tanzania Village Development Project was placed. The funding for this project is channeled directly to the regional level. Although technical assistance is provided for help in some areas of project planning and management, the basic structure for development in the region was found to be sufficiently well organized that no new organizations, committees or other structures were designed into the project.

Ethiopia, Ghana and Upper Volta

In three other countries -- Ethiopia, Ghana and Upper Volta -- it was concluded that enough authority had devolved upon subnational entities that a decentralized approach to project management could be attempted. In Ethiopia, a great deal of power and authority has been granted to the provincial administration and, at a lower level, to peasant associations. In Ghana, District Councils have been created and designated as the primary political/administrative entities of their districts, with certain powers of taxation. In Upper Volta, Regional Development Organizations (ORDs) have been established that are independent from control of both regional governments and regional line ministries.

In none of these cases is local control over development activities as complete (or as tested) as in Tanzania. The power of the governor in Ethiopia is derived from his appointment by the Dergue. In Ghana, the District Councils so far lack any control over the funds or the personnel of line ministries.

Some central government agencies, notably the Public Works Department, have more or less ignored the District Councils and continue to pursue their activities in much the same way as before decentralization. In Upper Volta the ORDs have been established as separate from, rather than integrated with, the regional governments. Nevertheless, the very existence of these organizations, with their intimate knowledge of and natural links to local realities, made them attractive candidates for implementing organizations.

Thus primary implementation responsibility for the Ghana District Development Project, the Upper Volta Women's Project and the Ethiopia Rehabilitation Project was located at subnational levels in their respective countries. Because of the tenuous and untested capacities of the subnational organizations, however, certain safeguards were written into each project. In Ghana the PP recognized explicitly that it might become necessary to identify "alternative organizational arrangements for promoting local development." In Ethiopia one of the project outputs is to be the creation of a Provincial Development Office. In Upper Volta - WP the ORDs share implementation responsibilities with the National Women's Council and with the Domestic Economy Unit in the national government.

Controlling Line Ministries

Another common problem with attempts at decentralized implementation is that subnational units of government find it difficult to gain control over the line ministries operating within their region, province or district. The administrative structures in Kenya and Tanzania are illustrative of two different approaches to resolving this problem. In Kenya there is a district government structure, with the Commissioner deriving his authority from the Office of the President. A District Development Officer, recruited and trained by the Ministry of Finance and Planning but reporting to the Office of the President, is responsible for coordinating line ministry activities and planning local assistance projects from a special development fund. But the line ministries maintain control over their own staff and funding and continue their largely autonomous planning and execution of nationally scheduled programs. As a result, the attempts at district-level coordination of development activities in Kenya have met with little success.[6]

In Tanzania, the Regional Development Director derives his authority from the Prime Minister's Office, and line agencies also plan for and spend the majority of the development funds in any one geographic area. The authority of the regional chief is such, however, that the major planning efforts are coordinated at his district/regional level, and the line agencies expect and receive bottom-up planning. In Tanzania development assistance funds complement overall district planning efforts; they do not merely fill small gaps in the preprogrammed efforts of line ministries, as in Kenya.

In sum, turning over operational responsibility for a project to a subnational entity (e.g., a provincial, regional or district government, a local development organization, or a decentralized, semi-autonomous government agency) has the advantage of bringing operational decisionmaking closer to "ground level." It may also make it possible to concentrate the control of resources in one organization, but more often this function is split at the local level, posing difficult problems of coordination and cooperation. A common problem is that overall capabilities and experience in rural development -- on both institutional and individual dimensions -- are less developed at lower administrative levels. Another problem is that decentralizing authority for development decisionmaking does not obviate the necessity for integrating local development plans into overall national planning. Decentralization of authority over a project poses a jurisdictional threat to previously powerful line ministries. It may also pose a threat to host country or AID officials who insist on strict controls over project activities, particularly in the accounting area.

Working Through Integrated Development Agencies

If the line ministries cannot do the job, and decentralization is not yet feasible, allowable, or administratively practicable, another approach is to work through integrated development agencies. These agencies often derive their authority directly from the Prime Minister or a President's office, and are given direct responsibility to implement or to coordinate the implementation of rural development projects in specified areas.

In the Republic of Senegal, for example, the government has divided the country into six agro-ecological zones (e.g., a peanut basin zone, a delta zone for irrigated agriculture, a cotton zone) and has created an equal number of public enterprises to manage rural development schemes in those zones. These enterprises enjoy a degree of financial autonomy, flexibility in administrative procedures, and freedom in recruitment and control over staff that has increased their efficiency in delivery of services.

Afghanistan, Upper Volta and Niger

Three of the twelve projects under review -- Afghanistan, Upper Volta - OP and Niger -- were designed in countries where some variant of this approach was possible.

In Afghanistan the Rural Development Department (RDD), operating under the Prime Minister, has the authority to implement development programs in pilot districts. For those functions that deal directly with development, RDD undertakes the responsibilities of all line ministries. To do this, RDD hires and pays teachers, agricultural extensionists, doctors and nurses, research station personnel, cooperative development specialists, and other locally based staff who were previously provided by the line ministries.

The DAI team, supported by the AID Mission, argued that a different arrangement was preferable for the Afghanistan project. Rather than have RDD usurp all rural functions of the line ministries -- a move that seemed administratively unreasonable as well as politically unviable as the project moved beyond a few pilot districts to the country as a whole -- it was suggested that RDD should serve as a coordinating mechanism to ensure that the line ministries did a better job, and one that was integrated into an overall district development plan. It was proposed that planning take place at the provincial level, under the authority of the Governor and an RDD staff unit, whose chief would serve as the "development" officer for the province.

Predictably, this suggestion was resisted by RDD itself. The RDD President wanted control over all funds, personnel and resources going into a district development program, arguing that this would speed the process of development. DAI and the Mission agreed that this arrangement would bring faster development to the pilot district, but felt it would not provide a replicable model for district development throughout Afghanistan, since RDD either could not or would not be allowed (by the political pressure of the line ministries) to usurp all functions of government in all districts of the country.

In Upper Volta - OP and the Niger Department Development Project, similar problems arose. In Upper Volta - OP, a project designed to promote alternative income-generating activities in resettlement villages, the implementing agency is the Volta Valley Authority (AVV), which has responsibility for all development activities in the resettlement areas. Here the problem is that Upper Volta's Regional Development Organizations (ORDs) operate in areas surrounding the resettlement areas, and it made little sense to duplicate staff, resources and activities between organizations pursuing similar objectives and operating in adjacent territories. In Niger, the National Union of Cooperatives and Credit (UNCC) was named to supervise departmental and arrondissement-level development activities. These activities are to be carried out by development committees, composed of line ministry representatives at each level. Here the obvious problem is what authority the UNCC will have at its disposal to promote the necessary cooperation between line ministries.

Lead Line Agencies in The Philippines

Another project, which DAI assisted, illustrates one more variant of the "integrated development organization" approach and its attendant problems. In this integrated regional program -- the Bicol River Basin Development Project in the Philippines[7] -- lead line agencies were tapped for the chore of integrating the activities of local line ministries in each subproject. The lead line agency designated for each subproject depended upon the focus and thrust of the development activities in question.

In one subproject, for example, the irrigation department was designated as the lead line agency. Other line agencies working the area had agreed to cooperate and coordinate activities with the irrigation department, but each letter of formal agreement had a slightly different specification of what was to be seconded or shared. There was to be incentive pay for field personnel, but this measure has not been approved and activated. Moreover, the incentive pay became a prime candidate for elimination during a period when budget cutting became necessary. All in all, there were few if any incentives to promote coordination, mutual planning, joint scheduling, or assignment of personnel. The regional commission could expend or withhold major development funds and complete planning activities, but when it came to operation, the field workers were controlled by and responsibile to their home line agencies.

In working through organizations that have been created for the precise purpose of "integrating" rural development activities, it is sometimes possible to enjoy institutional competence and experienced personnel. Sometimes, too, these organizations have strong authority to coordinate activities in specified geographic areas. More often, however, these organizations have limited authority, limited institutional and staff experience, and run up against the power and prerogatives of traditional line ministries. It is in these cases in particular that mechanisms and procedures for coordination must be created during project design in order to minimize problems of organizational rivalries and bottlenecks during implementation.

Creating Special Project Management Units

If host country organization, administraion, and institutional capability are too weak to support rural development activities, a last option is to create a special project management unit. This is the approach frequently chosen by the World Bank for the rural development projects it supports. It reflects a strong desire for early benefits and bankable returns from project activities, but less concern for the self-perpetuation of project benefits once foreign assistance is withdrawn.[8]

Among the twelve projects, only in Zaire did there seem to be no alternative but to establish a special project management unit (PMU). The governmental apparatus in the project area was not simply neutral in its impact on the rural populations; in some cases it was sharply negative. As a condition of funding, the project designers obtained an agreement from the GOZ to dismantle or dismiss some of the organizations and individuals who were extorting, rather than assisting, the small farmers in the project area. The project, however, calls for local government organizations to assume increasing responsibility for the project over time. This is to ensure that the activities and responsibilities of the project, initiated by the PMU, will be institutionalized under regular government authority prior to the end of the project. Since the project will take over the functions of the regular government line agencies in North Shaba, at start-up it will pose a serious threat to local officials. Strong national-level support, which to date has been forthcoming, will be needed to ensure that the PMU survives and will be able to implement the project effectively.

BUILDING FLEXIBILITY AND REDESIGN CAPACITY INTO PROJECT MANAGEMENT

The capacity of organizations to carry out development activities must be assessed in several areas. Some of these (e.g., management experience, technical expertise, accounting ability, personnel policies) are necessary in virtually any organization, whatever its endeavor. Their presence does not suffice to guarantee flexibility, however, in organizations involved in rural development activities.

Many development organizations are quite capable from administrative and technical points of view. But there is another skill that is more often missing and that needs to be developed: this is the capacity to _design flexibility_ into development plans and programs and tolerate it in implementation. This is a critical capacity, because development projects are rarely able to follow blueprint designs. There is inevitable change, redirection, and replanning accompanying almost all such projects. The need for continual and iterative redesign of project activities is, in most cases, not only inevitable but desirable, for development is basically a process of promoting change, and change by its nature often comes about in unexpected ways an at unexpected times.

At first glance the problem of trying to create a capacity for flexibility in an institutionalized environment seems insoluble. Bureaucracies are inherently conservative, adaptive rather than innovative, and committed to institutional maintenance and incrementalism rather than output and rapid change.[9] Yet by understanding the problem in more detail and in a development context, some approaches, if not outright solutions, emerge.

Planning, Programming, Monitoring, and Evaluation

In the process approach to project development, overall planning and the selection and scheduling of discrete project activities are based on an assessment of the resources and development potential of an area. These planning and programming activities, moreover, take place during project implementation and are carried out in collaboration with members of the target population. Critical individual and organizational skills that are needed for planning, programming, monitoring, and evaluation include an ability to identify information needed about an area, an ability to collect and analyze data to satisfy identified information requirements, and an ability to collaborate effectively with the local population. Furthermore, a flexibility to redesign and reschedule activities is built into projects through the use of management information systems and close monitoring and periodic evaluations of project activities.

The skill most often lacking in implementing organizations is the ability to identify or appreciate the need for certain types of information concerning a target area and target population. Particularly unappreciated by many host country organizations is the need to understand sociocultural, socioeconomic, and organizational structures, and to identify differences in farming systems within an area.[10] This problem is a delicate one for expatriate project designers to bring up, because local officials understandably take umbrage at the suggestion that they do not "know" their area. The problem is not so much that local officials _lack_ knowledge, as it is that their knowledge is not _structured_ in a way that makes it useful for planning and programming project activities.[11]

The ability to collect and analyze data to satisfy information requirements is also limited in most host country implementing organizations, although the personnel of candidate organizations frequently do have the skills around which data collection and analysis ability can be built. Many ministries and other government organizations have extension or other outreach personnel who routinely gather information of various sorts (e.g., use of agricultural inputs and credit, sales of farm products) from rural populations. Many also have personnel with data analysis skills such as statistics and computer programming. With proper technical assistance, other skills -- sampling, the use of questionnaires and standardized farm records, multivariate analysis -- can be added in rather straightforward ways to organizational skill banks.

One critical failing of many implementing institutions is that information, even if well specified, well collected and well analyzed, is not _used_ in ways that facilitate reiterative planning and programming. There are many reasons for this. Sometimes information is not gathered quickly enough or at the right time to enter into the calculus of critical decisions. Sometimes the right information is not channeled to the right source. Sometimes key decisionmakers are so overwhelmed with information that they are not able to digest it or use it in any meaningful way.

The question is also complicated by organizational dynamics. Many Third World organizations are run in an authoritarian and autocratic fashion. Often the man at the top makes all the important decisions. The role of subordinates is to carry out instructions rather than contribute to the decisions on which those instructions are based. Subordinates may, therefore, sit on information rather than use it or channel it to the decisionmakers.

Still another problem is the failure of many organizations to appreciate the connection between monitoring and evaluation on the one hand, and planning and programming on the other. Many organizations consider decisions, once made, as set in concrete. Monitoring activities and periodic evaluations are seen either as threats or as opportunities for justification of past activities, rather than as tools to help redesign and redirect activities that have gone off course.

Some of these problems were found, in greater or lesser degree, in each of the organizations designated as primary implementing agencies for the twelve projects. In all twelve projects, some type of technical assistance and/or training was recommended for the purpose of helping organizations to create more rational information and decisionmaking systems. The technical assistance would be used for several purposes. One would be to reorient decisionmaking from autocratic direction-giving toward collaborative problem-solving. Another would be to advise counterparts in data identification, data gathering and data analysis procedures. For this purpose, it was recommended in several projects that implementing organizations establish management information systems for monitoring and evaluation of project activities. Technical assistants would then guide the organization in the programming uses of information obtained through the monitoring and evaluation processes.

The Use of Monitoring and Evaluation to Support Project Implementation

In each of the twelve projects, a formal explanation was given of an ongoing monitoring and evaluation system -- an information system that would be at the disposal of project management. These systems have certain common characteristics. Project field staff are in regular contact with the target population. The desired impact of the project is identified as behavior changes on the part of the target population, with respect to production techniques or other socioeconomic factors. With a carefully designed fill-in-the-blocks instrument, field personnel are able to bring back reports to project management on what change or lack of change is taking place. This information then flags problems in need of resolution. With slightly more structure and investigation, the reasons for the problems can be identified, and solutions recommended to the management unit charged with making the project work.

The state of the art in information systems is such that simple approaches can be used with excellent results: formal incorporation of local participants in project committees, regular meetings with project participants and field staff, and careful attempts to build two-way communications with the leadership of the rural population. A generally forgotten but extremely useful tactic in seeking reasons that a project might show less than desirable success is simply to ask those members of the target population not being reached by the project why they are not participating.

If more complex and statistically valid information systems are to be incorporated into a project, handbooks, manuals and prescriptions become useless. There are no proven or documented successes in this difficult field. The tendency is to design overcomplex systems that generate very large data banks, never to be used in project decisionmaking. Costs of this information generation and retrieval can be very high. The use of census-type surveys and multipurpose household surveys has given very spotty results.[12] AID has made few funds available for experimentation with alternative data collection and analysis systems to support rural development. The World Bank has been similarly parsimonious.

One proposed USAID-supported project in the Philippines, the Economic and Social Impact Assessment project to be undertaken in cooperation with the Philippine National Economic Development Agency, would provide funds and specialists to test alternative data collection methods (e.g., statistical surveys, collection by field staff, simple indicators, farm records). This would be a major step forward in assistance to harried project managers who are admonished to keep their projects flexible and to use data from their successes and failures to redesign their priorities and approaches, without knowing how this can be done cheaply and efficiently, or understanding what it will take to determine the costs and benefits of additional and more precise information. This is an item on the agenda of support to rural development projects that has not been sufficiently addressed.

PROJECT DECISIONMAKING STRUCTURE

Most development projects involve complex clusters of activities requiring decisions and actions from a variety of institutional and individual sources. To arrive at optimal organizational arrangements for project implementation, it is not sufficient merely to identify a capable host country institution and assign it full responsibility for project implementation. Such an action ignores the fact that the designated "implementing agency" generally has other projects and activities that will compete with the new assignment for the organization's priorities, interests, and resources. Beyond this, the implementing agency will not have complete control over all activities and decisions, no matter how powerful it is. It will inevitably depend upon and be affected by the decisions and actions of other organizations.

During project design, it is useful to identify various types of decisions that will be made during implementation and to match these decision-types to the organizations that will make them. Procedures and mechanisms can then be devised that will help induce decisions favorable to project objectives.

Policy Decisions

Policy decisions are usually not made by the organization assigned responsibility for implementing the project; yet many policy decisions will critically affect chances for project success. In the Chile project, a policy decision by the government to make and continue a subsidy to farmers for their use of technical service units became a critical element in project design. The success of the Zaire project will depend to a great extent on the firmness with which the GOZ supports the autonomy and the authority of the project management unit in the project area. In Ghana, much will depend on the GOG's commitment to its plans for decentralizing development decisionmaking at the district level. In Haiti, an important determinant of project success will be the GOH's overall commitment to agricultural and rural development, and its more specific decisions concerning subsidies for agricultural inputs and price supports and tax policy for agricultural products, particularly coffee.

During the design process, AID generally obtains a commitment from the host country government to foot twenty-five percent of project costs.[13] This is usually cited as a concrete indicator of government support for the project. But it is one thing to get a limited commitment before a project starts up and quite another to maintain a working commitment that will support project activities. It is often necessary to set up special mechanisms or "lobbies" within the government.

In Chile, the project established a National Commission for Technical Assistance to ensure that appropriate and timely decisions and actions could be obtained from the various agencies of the Ministry of Agriculture and other government agencies. In Zaire, an attempt was made to marshall the interest and support of the central government by establishing two national-level committees. The first, a Project Steering Committee, is essentially a political committee set up to provide high-level policy and program guidance. The second, a Project Liaison Staff Committee, which is composed of representatives of the Department of Agriculture, the National Cereals Office, the Office of Political Affairs, the Office of Roads, and the Department of Finance, was established to provide specific action backstopping for the project at the national level.

The primary reason for setting up these committees and special mechanisms is to create an interest group for the project among policymakers and other high-level decisionmakers. Such mechanisms serve to maintain project visibility and to lobby for positive decisions and actions that will help the project operationally.

Local Participation in Decisionmaking

By now it is well documented that a critical determinant of success in area development projects is local participation in decisionmaking for project design and implementation. A good project design will identify or create organizational arrangements that facilitate this participation and promote two-way communications between the project and its intended beneficiaries.

In most cases, it is possible to work through existing governmental or local organizational arrangements to promote participation. In Ethiopia, the project design provided that direct links be established between the Provincial Development Office and the newly formed peasant associations. In Ghana, the District Council, which is to become the implementing agency for the project, has a built-in local participation arrangement since one-third of its members are selected by village associations and other traditional authorities. In Niger, the design provided that project participants be represented on area development committees, which will in turn have formal participation in arrondissement-level development committees.

In some cases, mechanisms to promote local participation have to be created. In Upper Volta - OP local organizations were scarce, since the target areas consisted of recently established resettlement villages; but the project design required that the villages establish an organization to receive and manage a revolving loan fund. Extensive interviews with small farmers in the resettlement villages indicated that they would be willing and eager to establish such organizations; the interviews also provided several ideas for potential development activities for which the funds would be used.

Once established, the organizations must be invested with sufficient power and standing to make their voices heard and their opinions felt. This is complicated by the fact that, in many countries, like Ghana, a deliberate attempt has been made to create a civil service that is insulated from local pressures. While this may enhance greater professionalism and honesty among civil servants, it also means that these government officials cannot be held accountable for their actions by those who most directly suffer the consequences of their mistakes.

There are several specific ways to vest local organizations with sufficient power or influence to control project activities and to make government officials answerable to them. Some of the more common include:

- Giving voting representation on development committees, district councils or specific work groups to members of local organizations;

- Giving sign-off or veto power to village or other traditional groups for specific activities that would directly affect them;

- Having farmer groups keep a record of extension worker visits; and

- Establishing advisory groups with membership from local organizations that would periodically monitor and review project progress.

Imagination and specific local circumstances are the only constraints to creating a long list of such mechanisms to promote local participation in concrete ways. Informal structures, spontaneous meetings and the like can often serve best the purpose of getting the various bureaucratic and local interest groups to appreciate the mutual interests they have in working through community organizations in development planning and implementation. The overall point is that such mechanisms and structures should be introduced into a project design in order to promote optimal local participation during implementation.

As contacts are established and mechanisms set up to include target population groups in project decisionmaking, a deliberate attempt should be made to include representatives from the designated implementing agency in the meetings and discussions with villagers. This will serve not only to establish contacts and begin a process of two-way communication, but in a more elemental sense, it will ensure that the poorer members of the area's population become "visible" to extension workers and other officials in the implementing agency, a phenomenon not to be taken for granted.[14]

Operational Decisions

The operational level is that level where most of the everyday action- and problem-oriented project decisions are made. It is here that the work of the project is done, that tasks are assigned, schedules drawn up, resources allocated and activities carried out. The remainder of this section will deal with two organizational problems that commonly arise at the operational level.

Diffusion of Operational Responsibility

A problem that commonly arises is that responsibility for carrying out discrete project activities, along with the resources to do so, is diffused among a number of government agencies or at different levels of government. This usually happens because the project involves a great variety of activities (e.g., credit, extension, marketing, public works, training) that fall naturally in the domains of a corresponding number of existing government agencies. Sometimes domestic politics of the host country dictate that development monies be distributed among government agencies.

Such diffused operational responsibilities inevitably lead to great problems in coordination, leading to delays, inefficiencies and wasted resources. This type of situation is illustrated by the experience of the Haiti Small Farmer Coffee Project, an ongoing project evaluated by DAI in 1977.[15]

Bicephalous Management in Haiti. At the operational level, implementation responsibilities for the Small Farmer Coffee Project are divided primarily between two Haitian organizations, a Coffee Institute (IHPCADE) and an Agricultural Credit Bureau (BCA). At the time of the DAI evaluation, when the project had been underway for two and one-half years, there was no project manager, although it was informally understood that the Director of IHPCADE functioned in that role. A "project coordinating committee," composed of representatives from various agencies in the Ministry of Agriculture and other GOH ministries and agencies, was given a loose mandate to coordinate the activities of IHPCADE and BCA.

It was relatively clear that BCA is responsible for the credit component of the project, while IHPCADE is responsible for all other project activities. Operationally, however, a number of problems have arisen with respect to the coordination of the credit and other project activities. Such problems have been particularly acute with respect to formation of and interaction with farmer credit groups, the selection and delivery of agricultural inputs, and the programming and supervision of credit, extension and other activities. One concrete example is that the annual fertilizer procurements, an IHPCADE responsibility, are ostensibly based on actual orders for fertilizer made by small farmer credit groups, whose formation is a BCA responsibility. In practice the annual procurement has taken place months before most of the credit organizations were formed, so that in some years there may be a surplus of fertilizer while in others there may not be enough to meet demand.

It was clear to the DAI evaluation team, as well as to most participants, that the project's operational problems stemmed largely from the bicephalous (even acephalous) nature of the project's management structure. Local BCA agents take their directives from and report to BCA headquarters in Port-au-Prince; local IHPCADE agents take their directives from and report to IHPCADE headquarters in Port-au-Prince. No regular meetings between these agencies take place, at either the national or the local levels. When there are informal meetings, agendas are nonspecific, discussions are undirected, and decisions are vague or not made at all. The project coordinating committee has no clear-cut responsibilities, meets infrequently, and in any case is too large and unwieldy to manage the project operations effectively.

Three possible solutions to this management problem presented themselves. The first and most extreme was to cut out one of the agencies, BCA, from further participation in the project, transferring responsibility for credit activities to IHPCADE (a function which IHPCADE had performed in the past). This suggestion met with predictable resistance from BCA, which argued that Haiti needed a viable agricultural credit organization and that if the coffee project portfolio was taken away from BCA, the organization would be weakened by the loss of capital.[16] A second suggestion was that BCA open a special credit window for the project and second some of its staff to IHPCADE to manage the credit operations. In this way BCA would not lose the coffee project account and would also have its own staff trained in the group lending procedures that were a part of the project. This suggestion was also resisted on the grounds that a "bank" (actually both IHPCADE and BCA are agencies of the Ministry of Agriculture) could not turn over decisionmaking authority on loans to another agency. BCA was also concerned that seconding staff would weaken its own personnel position. A third suggestion, in effect a compromise, was to name a "project manager" within the Ministry of Agriculture to supervise or coordinate the activities of the two agencies. This solution is better than none at all, but is decidedly third-best, since it involves creating an artificial post with no history (hence no institutional credits or debts) and no staff, to be put in a position of quasi-authority over two strong agencies with their own budgets, their own priorities and their own ways of doing things.

Acephalous Management in Mali. Another example of diffused responsibilities in a project design is provided by the Mali Rural Works Project, which at this writing is between the design and implementation stages. This project is designed to promote participation in the development of rural works among the residents of some 200 villages in Mali. Administratively, "responsibility" for discrete activities is assigned to various levels of social and political organization, starting with the village and progressing upward to the district, the county and the region. Project personnel (Malian and expatriate) are to be assigned to each of these levels to "coordinate" project activities at that level. Overall "coordination" between concerned central agencies will be provided by the Ministry of Rural Development at the national level. Requests for funding approval for subproject activities will be transmitted up this hierarchy with final approval coming from the AID Country Development Officer in Bamako.

In its concern with building the project from the ground up and with forging links with key levels of government and key organizations, the project design has demonstrated an understanding of some of the problems that may arise if specific mechanisms are not designed to ensure the cooperation of all interested and involved parties. Substantively, the project seems quite sound. However, there is a characteristic lack of specificity about which level of government or which organization will have primary implementation responsibility for the project.

The design documents do not clearly designate a particular organization to exercise operational control over project personnel (e.g., hiring, firing, assigning tasks, evaluation of performance) and over the project budget (e.g., disbursing funds, meeting project costs, including contingencies). Unless some arrangement is made to centralize these responsibilities and resources in a particular organization, it can be safely predicted that the Mali Rural Works Project will suffer critical delays and administrative inefficiencies.

The Lesson. The lesson to be learned from these examples is that, notwithstanding the need to deal with an overall decisionmaking structure, the smooth operation of most projects requires that, to the extent possible, a single organization (or level of government) be assigned principal responsibility for operational or day-to-day project activities. The designated organization should have the authority to program activities, assign tasks, allocate resources, supervise (or actually carry out) most of the work, and deal with problems as they arise. In order to carry out its tasks effectively, the designated organization should also be given operational control over most project resources.

Coordination of Project Activities

As the Haiti case illustrated, political pressures and other circumstances sometimes make it impossible to centralize authority and resources for project operations in one organization. Even when most authority and most resources are centralized, there frequently remains some residual control over operational project decisions exercised by other organizations.[17] When this is the case, there is a need to create mechanisms and procedures to promote effective coordination.

The world "coordination" is itself one of the most abused in the development liturgy. Too often a design ends with a plea for coordination, rather than with incentives or procedures for promoting it. As Robert Chambers has written:

> ...the word 'co-ordination' provides a handy means for avoiding responsibility for clear proposals. It is perhaps for this reason that it is much favored by visiting missions who are able to conceal their ignorance of how an administrative system works or what might be done about it by identifying 'a need for better co-ordination.' Indeed, a further research project of interest would be to test the hypothesis that the value of reports varies inversely with the frequency with which the word 'co-ordination' is used.[18]

For a design team, the first step in creating mechanisms to promote coordination must be to gain a thorough understanding of the way the current host country system works. The specific information needed will differ by project and by country, but for virtually all projects a good start can be made by obtaining answers to the following questions:

1. Who has sign-off authority over money? Power and authority in most administrations flow from those who control the use of money; identifying the individual(s) who determine how money is spent in situations similar to that of the project can lead quickly to an understanding of mechanisms and procedures

that might be needed to ensure a smooth flow of funding into project activities.

2. <u>What are the incentives for good performance and what are the sanctions for poor performance among potential project personnel?</u> Project success ultimately depends on the performance of people. It is critical to understand, therefore, what motivates potential project personnel. Who controls salary increases and promotions and what do workers have to do to earn them?

Once some understanding has been reached of the way the existing system works, concrete measures can be taken to promote coordination among potentially competing or hostile agencies. In general, there are two ways of dealing with this problem during design. The first is to create <u>incentives</u> for people and institutions to work together. Incentives to carry out the project as designed must be stronger than pressures that support other (often traditional) patterns of behavior. These incentives may include salary adjustments, the chance to control more funds or more staff, or the promise of career promotion, or they may involve agreements or even specific "contracts" by which organizations are assured that cooperation with another organization will not mean loss of authority, personnel, or funding. The second is to specify <u>procedures</u> by which coordination will take place. Too often, project designs simply state that "coordination will take place" between agency X and agency Y. Rather than dismiss this important problem with generalities, it is preferable to spell out the coordination procedures. These might include regular meetings for selecting activities, for programming resources, and for review of field reports. They might also include the specification of whatever work groups might need to be established to tackle special problems.

CONCLUSIONS

The experience gained in the design of the twelve projects, and in a number of other project evaluations, has demonstrated that arriving at optimal organizational arrangements for project implementation is a demanding and difficult, but very necessary, exercise. Organizational factors are critical to project success and should carry equal weight with technical and economic considerations in project design.

Organizational arrangements for each project must be tailored to fit the host country's administrative/political setup and the objectives and expected outputs of the project. In the twelve projects under review, four strategies were used to arrive at optimal organizational arrangements.

- Working through traditional line ministries;
- Working through subnational government entities;
- Working through integrated development agencies; and
- Creating special project management units.

There are many variants of these four approaches, as well as other general approaches that can be used to arrive at optimal organizational arrangements for project implementation. Trade-offs and compromises are inevitably necessary to obtain host country and donor support for any particular arrangement, since the outcome of the arrangements will determine who controls project resources. From a development point of view, it may be preferable, for example, to work through decentralized units of government and to centralize the control of project resources in one organization, but, for political or institutional reasons, neither of these options may be available.

Whatever structural arrangements are arrived at, there remain two behavioral problems that must be addressed. One is the problem of cooperation among development organizations and the other is the capacity within organizations to cope with flexible project designs. Neither incentives to cooperate nor the capacity to be flexible can be assumed; rather they must be built into a good project design. Precise methods of building in these features should be the subject of further cross-project research.

NOTES

[1] Several ideas here have been generated by George H. Honadle, a senior institutional analyst with DAI. See George H. Honadle, "Anticipating Roadblocks in Organizational Terrain: How Development Project Organization Design Makes a Difference," DAI and

Syracuse University, 1977.

[2] For a discussion of traditional organization through line ministries at the national level see F. Kramer, *Perspectives on Public Bureaucracy,* New York: W. W. Norton, 1975.

[3] For a discussion of decentralization and organization at the subnational level, see Ira Sharkansky, *Spending in the American Cities,* Chicago: Rand McNally, 1968.

[4] Guy Hunter, *Modernizing Peasant Societies,* London: Oxford University Press, 1969, p. 203.

[5] Not surprisingly, the countries with the most viable rural institutions and the most effective decentralization are also those whose governments have placed high priority on agricultural and rural development and were rated accordingly on their overall commitment to the "New Directions" of AID (Table 8.1).

[6] Peter F. Weisel, "Some Issues Related to District Development (in Kenya)," Kenya Ministry of Finance and Planning and Development Alternatives, Inc., March 1977. Dr. Weisel was completing a two-year assignment in Kenya when this paper was written.

[7] See George H. Honadle, "Implementing Integrated Area Development in the Bicol," a report to the U.S. Agency for International Development and the Bicol River Basin Coordinating Committee, Development Alternatives, Inc., October 25, 1977. See also Charles F. Sweet, "The Bicol River Basin Development Project: Some Preliminary Observations," a discussion paper prepared for the Bicol River Basin Coordinating Committee and Program Office, Development Alternatives, Inc., October 7, 1977.

[8] See Gary Brewer, *Politicians, Bureaucrats, and Consultants,* New York: Basic Books, 1975, for a thorough discussion on methods of creating special management units to implement projects.

[9] For a good discussion of the problems of development administration, see B. B. Schaffer, "The Deadlock in Development Administration," in Colin Leys, ed., *Politics and Change in Developing Countries,* London: Cambridge University Press, 1969, pp. 177-211.

[10] In North Shaba, for example, there are three distinct tribal groups and half a dozen identifiably different farming practices. For a more thorough discussion of information requirements for project design and implementation, see Chapter 6.

[11] An absolute lack of knowledge about local conditions is more often a problem when a national-level rather than a local-level organization is assigned implementation responsibilities.

[12] See Development Alternatives, Inc., *Information for Decisionmaking in Rural Development*, op. cit.

[13] Under the AID system, the twenty-five percent host country commitment can usually be calculated from contributions in the private sector of land, labor, and materials, or from the public sector in seconded staff and staff support.

[14] In a random sample survey of small farmers in Kenya, conducted by extension workers who worked in the area, many of the extension workers complained that the sample included too few progressive farmers. The workers were surprised and startled at the many poor people they were forced to visit. See Robert Chambers, *Managing Rural Development,* Uppsala: The Scandinavian Institute of African Studies, 1974, p. 80.

[15] See Development Alternatives, Inc., "Evaluation of the Haiti Small Farmer Coffee Project," prepared for the Office of Development Resources, Latin America Bureau, AID, June 1977.

[16] The counter argument is that institution building for its own sake (i.e., in the absence of any proof that the institution is doing an effective job) should not take priority over getting benefits to a target population. In a country like Haiti, however, when it comes to a power struggle between the organized interests of a government agency and the unorganized interests of small farmers, it is clear that the former will win.

[17] For a discussion of the problems of coordinating agencies to implement projects in the United States, see Richard Nathan, *The Administrative Presidency*, 1976.

[18] Robert Chambers, op. cit., pp. 24-25.

9
Reflections on the Review/Approval Process

Chapter 3 identified the major problems encountered by the twelve projects as they moved through the AID project review/approval system. The purpose of this chapter is to move beyond that empirical approach to a more general consideration of what might be done to make the AID system more efficient. These reflections begin with a discussion of the system as it operated during the period when the twelve projects were being developed, and proceed to an examination of some alternative approaches to improving that system. The chapter concludes by analyzing the particular requirements of process approach projects in terms of their movement through the review/approval system.

PROBLEMS WITH THE EXISTING REVIEW/APPROVAL SYSTEM

In order to interpret the way the AID review/approval system has functioned, it is useful to characterize the roles of the principal actors: AID/Washington, the Mission and the host countries. During the period when most of the twelve projects came up for review, and until the recently initiated AID reorganization, authority was divided along the following lines: The primary responsibility of AID/Washington was to ensure that the Agency complied with Congressional mandates, while the Missions were responsible for using those mandates as guidelines for project selection. Ideally the host country was expected to initiate projects or at least to collaborate with the Mission in the selection process.

Although these responsibilities were generally acknowledged, in practice the division functioned unsatisfactorily.[1] Disagreements frequently developed over project selection criteria, and over how to evaluate projects for conformity with Congressional mandates. While debate over general development philosophy persisted, no clearly defined Agency regulations were available to resolve major disagreements.

These difficulties meant high decision costs for projects moving through the AID review/approval system. As explained in Chapter 3, these costs were manifested in long delays between submission and approval of project proposals.[2] They represented a serious drain on the Agency's resources, but most important, there was no solid evidence that the delays had a positive effect on project quality. The case of the Ghana project is especially troubling, since there was broad support for the project and the approach that was being used, and still the project took over two years to move through the system. Indeed, this agonizing process is not complete even now: twenty months after the submission of the PRP, which contained the substance of the project, no contractor had been selected to implement the project.

Even when project review led to prompt approval, there was no sure indication that the system was fulfilling its prescribed functions. Four of the twelve projects "sailed through," with one month or less elapsing between the submission of the Project Paper and its approval by AID/Washington.[3] In all four cases, however, serious issues remained outstanding, which could have been addressed during the review process and were not. In the review of the Haiti and Zaire projects, questions arose regarding the extent of the host country government's commitment to small farmer development. In the Chile and Colombia cases, there were uncertainties within the host country about the mode of implementation, but these were not introduced into the review process as issues likely to impinge on project success. The Colombia project is being implemented by a line agency that does not have the appropriate specialists or interest to follow the design; in Chile, the implementing institutions were selected at the last minute and did not participate in the design process.

It is significant that three of the four rapidly approved projects were submitted to the Latin America Bureau of AID/Washington. As noted in Chapter 3, approval authority within this Bureau is clearly vested in an Executive Committee, whereas in the Africa Bureau authority has been divided between committees operating at two levels. A second factor affecting the speed of review is the institutionalization of certain approval criteria within the Latin

America Bureau. Project Papers routinely include calculations of the economic rate of return (sometimes in the form of an appendix, rather than as an integral part of the text). These projections sometimes bear little or no relation to the realities of the project environment. However, they do appear to assist in getting projects through the review/approval system without a hitch.

Detailed economic returns over project costs were calculated for Haiti and Chile, and incorporated into the Project Papers.[4] The calculations for Chile were based on a small farmer computer program used in the Latin America Bureau, and were not available until after the final design of the project was completed. The calculations were clearly a device for accelerating the approval process, since the decision had already been made that the project was valuable, important and within AID's "New Directions" mandate. In a similar fashion, packaging considerations dictated the use of cost-benefit analysis in the final Haiti Project Paper: The projections appended to this document were based on data collected in an area bearing almost no resemblance to the region where the project was to be implemented.

These case histories illuminate the main characteristics of the Agency's review/approval system. In its present form that system demands Project Papers that are essentially advocacy documents, written to persuade doubters. When such projections as rates of return, benefit-cost ratios, increases in target population income levels are included, they have no long-term value as guides to the evaluation of project performance in the implementation phase. They only serve the short-term function of securing approval within the AID bureaucracy, usually by anticipating the potential objections of special interest groups within the Agency.[5]

The twelve sample projects took an average of seven and a half months in the review/approval process (Table 5.3, page 122). If the four projects that were granted nearly instantaneous approval are omitted, the average time for the remaining eight was ten months. There are high costs to such delay, particularly in the diminishing enthusiasm of host country officials and their reduced commitment to release funds, staff, commodities and vehicles for project support. Such delays are also costly in terms of decreased enthusiasm on the part of the AID staff and others involved in the project.

While the costs of the present review and approval system are apparent, the benefits of extensive scrutiny are not easily identified. Two projects encountered substantive criticism. The Afghanistan project as designed was effectively dropped, following vigorous challenges mounted by NE/TECH. The Niger project was finally approved in the form originally advocated by the Mission Director, but only after long delays and disagreements. Neither AID/Washington's triumph in the Afghanistan case nor the field's victory in Niger can be considered a significant plus for the "New Directions" mandate. The decisions in each case could just as easily and rationally have been reversed. AID/Washington's role in the lengthy review of the two projects was neither constructive nor beneficial to the quality of either effort.

POSSIBLE REMEDIES FOR AN AILING SYSTEM

Two alternative methods come to mind for making the review/approval process more efficient: (1) maintaining the traditional division of authority, while attempting to clarify the rules of decisionmakers; or (2) transferring full decisionmaking authority to one source.

Maintaining the Traditional Division of Authority

The argument normally proposed in support of the first alternative runs as follows: AID/Washington, by proximity, is in the best position to interpret Congressional mandates and ensure that they are reflected in specific projects; and the Missions are similarly in the best position to articulate host country development priorities and intentions. It is clear that sharper delineation of approval roles between AID/Washington and the field would have moved at least some of the projects described in this report more rapidly through the review/approval system. To accomplish this objective, significant improvements would be needed in the definition of the chain of command (who is to make what decisions), the standardization of procedures (the activities, steps, sequence, content and format required for the submission of projects) and the definition of clear criteria for project selection (decision rules for decisionmakers).

Such proposed changes would not be easy to execute. There are many special interest groups in AID/Washington: technicians who believe that only agriculturalists can contribute to small farmer development projects, rural development specialists with a different understanding of technical assistance needs, environmentalists, health specialists, researchers, non-researchers, process approach designers and blueprint advocates. The representation of those interests in an ambiguous approval process has resulted in extended delays in project approval. Where procedures and selection criteria are uncertain or fluid, all actors have a chance to influence the decision, if only in a negative sense by preventing approval. Those who approve a project in the face of objections from others at the review table are in the exposed position. The doubters are seldom confronted with evidence from implemented projects that would refute their objections, precisely because AID has no systematic means of measuring project performance and impact.[6]

One approach would be to extend the method used in the Latin America Bureau to other bureaus in the Agency. With that method, the risk of long delays in project review is averted by applying a set of formulae to each project, and screening it carefully before it is submitted for approval. This in conjunction with considerable prior communication between the field and Washington effectively guarantees that a project will receive a stamp of approval when it is actually submitted, though it may reflect little more than the quality of the packaging. By adopting similar procedures, other bureaus could allocate funds, schedule project reviews, secure approval and obligate funds on a relatively fixed timetable.

One method of eliciting more efficient decision-making within the bureaus would be to fix deadlines for approval once Project Papers are submitted. Thus it might be decreeed that a project which has been submitted is automatically <u>rejected</u> within three months unless the bureau formally decides to approve it. Endless delays in approval pose no direct threat to members of the bureaucracy; on the other hand, a loss of funds or an inability to allocate funds reveals fumbling and indecisiveness, and puts those responsible in a position of accountability. A more expeditious and efficient review and approval process would almost certainly result from such a procedure. More projects would be moved into implementation, within a shorter time frame, than is presently the case. This would be an improvement over current practice, in the sense that bureaucratic logjams would not be allowed to form. However, this approach will not assure development projects of superior quality, since it affects only one segment of the AID system, and assumes no other basic changes in the other incentive structures of the Agency.

Even if the AID/Washington review and approval system were upgraded so that every bureau used the demonstrated most efficient procedures, other problems would remain unresolved. So long as AID/Washington holds the approval authority for projects, and simultaneously acts as the interpreter of Congressional desires that must be satisfied prior to project acceptance, requirements for documentation and annexes to the Project Papers will burgeon (analyzing social soundness, effects on women, environmental reviews, employment generation, nutritional consequences, income distribution, land tenure changes, and so forth).[7] The Regional Bureaus will continue to be caught between the policy directives from Congress and the real-world environment of the Missions. When there is a lack of fit, the exigencies of the approval process and the existing incentives to spend AID's funds will command the attention of the field staff and of the Regional Bureaus.

These are merely the logical consequences of placing the approval process in Washington. The first order of business in the Missions is to obtain development funds. If specific targets and future accomplishments must be incorporated in lengthy packaging and format (however unrealistic these may be) in order to obtain funds, this will continue to be the priority for all Mission activity. Without Project Papers that are devised to satisfy AID/Washington, there are no funds. Without funds, there is no country development program. The best and the brightest AID field staff are in the project design business.

The actual satisfaction of Congressional directives, as well as the demonstration of the efficacy of AID's "New Directions," lies in the implementation of development projects that deliver (as distinct from promise to deliver) benefits to the rural poor. To place the emphasis on up-front planning and justification of the design, when the state of the art in development assistance is such that there are no certain paths to follow, is a clear instance of misplaced priorities and incentives. AID/Washington can make no substantive contribution to the design of projects after the PP has been submitted. But the existing system concentrates the energies of the entire organization on the preparation for development assistance, rather than the results. Until such time as implementation is given priority; benefits are defined, measured and compared among projects; and results in the field become the hallmark of success within the Agency, the "New Directions" mandate will not fulfill its promise.

Transferring Decisionmaking Authority to the Field

During the recent and ongoing reorganization, the Agency has opted to delegate some increased authority to the Missions to plan, negotiate and formally approve small, experimental and PVO projects.

The decision to move greater responsibility to the field is also reflected in several administrative changes involving project development. In the area of project design, the system has been streamlined by moving to a two-paper sequence and consolidating requirements in order to eliminate duplication of analyses and descriptions. The elimination of the PRP was most important among these steps and facilitated the preparation of the design for the Tanzania Village Development Project.[8]

For the approval process, two mechanisms were established with the intention of achieving speedier decisions:

- The Accelerated Impact Program (AIP) was expanded to cover all African countries where AID programs were established. This procedure requires one Activity Identification Cable from the field, followed after fifteen days by a detailed Accelerated Activity Paper with AID/Washington approval authority vested in the Office of Regional Affairs;[9] and

- Mission Directors have been delegated the authority to approve projects (including PVO) costing up to $500,000, subject to Congressional Notification requirements.[10]

There has been considerable reaction, much of it positive, to this modest change in approval authority. However, a number of issues require further action. One party, who welcomed the change, voiced the following concern:

> ...we would sound a cautionary note for all concerned. Systems and procedures which developed under PBAR over the past few years were in response [to a] number [of] critical problems [with the] AID program. While these responses in themselves became so

> cumbersome, centralized and bureaucratized as to create new problems, we must not forget problems to which they responded. Burden[s] now are very much on Missions and Bureaus not to fall back on old sins, nor fail to develop adequate means [to] meet their new responsibilities.[11]

The actual degree of authority that has been delegated to the field remains an unresolved question. Detailed instructions have been promised on how much responsibility will be delegated and how it should be implemented, but they have only been vaguely outlined thus far. The delay is understandable since the questions to be examined are extremely complicated. But until they are addressed, the Missions cannot be expected to respond consistently to their new authority, nor to be thoroughly cognizant of the ramifications of their actions. For example, it appears that the Missions are not fully conversant with all the legislative requirements that must be fulfilled prior to the obligation of funds. Until this understanding is established, the General Counsel must take certain steps to ensure that the law is not being violated as the Mission Directors use the authority delegated to them.

Perhaps the greatest concern relates to the lack of Mission Director accountability for development results. The reorganization task force pointed out that the Agency:

> ...must eliminate the 'obligation of funds' as the prime factor in judging the effectiveness of field leaders. Development professionals should be judged on development results, not the amount of money obligated.[12]

The only way to produce this change in Mission Director incentives is to develop an AID capacity to evaluate the effectiveness of projects in achieving positive benefits for the rural poor. Then the policy bureau could concentrate on the actual results of projects under implementation rather than what projects should look like in the design phase. Effectiveness could then be determined, and Mission personnel and leadership could be judged, on the benefits delivered per unit of AID funding. Performance, implementation, collaboration and effective and viable development assistance would at least have the potential to replace unrealistic projections and large expenditures as criteria for approval in Project Papers.

Such an evaluation capability is within the state of the art in development assistance, but will not be achieved without devoting far more resources and staff to the problem than have previously been committed. Unless baseline data have been systematically assembled, it is not possible to examine a project that has been in existence for some years and attribute any changes in the target population to the intervention of development assistance. Without an understanding of the linkages among the local environment, the development resources being introduced, and any improvement in the quality of life of the target population, there is no way to measure and ascribe any change to the project.

One solution is to build into each project an information system that reports to project management on activities and their results. Much of this information can be obtained from project staff as they interact with the target population, particularly if paraprofessionals (e.g., paramedics, *promotores*, paratechnicians in agriculture) have been included in the project. An ongoing information system, which helps management correct the course of the project over time, combined with some special evaluation studies carried out at critical points in the project's life, can provide the data necessary for an assessment of project results. It may also, depending upon the methodology employed, explain why the results were high, low, or mixed in the project area.

There are few working models of such a system, simply because no major development assistance agency, including the World Bank, has been inclined to devote resources to the testing, refinement and placement of such systems in projects to be implemented. Our experience suggests that each system must be tailored to the specific project environment. The benefits of establishing such procedures could far outweigh the costs, particularly if the resultant evaluation capability is used to shift the emphasis within AID from design and approval to implementation.

A two-pronged approach to revisions in the present AID project development system would include:

- Transfer of project approval authority to the field; and

- Creation of an AID/Washington evaluation capability which could determine which project among those funded actually delivered benefits to the rural poor.

If the Missions had been able to exercise approval authority while the twelve projects described herein were being developed, AID would have benefited from:

- A significant percentage reduction in design time, since much effort now is expended on second-guessing the reviewers in regard to data requirements;
- A considerably improved project design, as time would be devoted to collaboration and to the details of host country and AID commitment (e.g., staff, funds, vehicles, commodities) during implementation; and
- A prompt start to implementation, within two months after completion of the design, rather than delays of up to two years.

This type of system would make it possible for designers working with the host country government to say that when satisfactory agreements have been reached, the approach determined, the actions to be taken specified, and the support detailed, the project *will* begin. This is very different from saying that, after the Project Paper is written, *if* Washington agrees, in eight months we might get a Project Agreement signed and in a year the project *might* begin. Such a change would reflect a new emphasis on the *implementation* of development projects.

RECOMMENDATIONS

In earlier chapters it has been argued that if projects are to benefit the rural poor, an evolutionary approach to project design and implementation offers the best chance for success. From a conceptual standpoint, there is no legitimate way to differentiate between design activities before and after implementation activities begin. The process approach calls for a continuing interaction between outsiders and potential project participants concerning design, redesign, and possible replication. Viewed from this standpoint, the current project review/approval process is an unnecessary encumbrance.

It is unrealistic, however, merely to suggest that the entire system be done away with for all types of projects. AID is responsible to the Congress, which is in turn responsible to the American taxpayer to ensure that foreign assistance monies are well spent. What then is called for when the process design/implementation approach is used? It is not always reasonable to demand detailed descriptions of what is to be done, how it is to be done, and what it will cost before giving approval to start the project. The answers are simply not available in all cases. Congress nevertheless requires, and legitimately so, adequate planning prior to the obligation of funds.

A two-phased review/approval process would seem warranted. The first phase of a process approach project would require a general statement of the project goal, the specifications of the area and target population, determination of an implementing organization within the host country, and a budget. Such a design must be thoughtful, but the design team does not necessarily require a great mass of information on the target area. A budget could be estimated that would allow a project to get underway in what might be called "pre-implementation," and sustain this effort for up to twenty-four months.[13] The responsibility for project approval in this first phase would rest with the Mission Director.

The use of Mission authority must be reasonable. It would make little sense if foundations for bridges were approved and funded in the pre-implementation stage, with the remainder of the construction scheduled for later, if and when a full project were approved.[14] The pre-implementation phase is to determine appropriate intervention into a society -- the answers to the who, why, where, when and how questions. It differs from a pilot program, in that the intention is to continue unless the project proves unimplementable as originally conceived or even with significant modifications and improvements during the second phase.

If authority to approve projects costing, for example, under two million dollars, and lasting under two years, were delegated to the Mission Directors under established guidelines, a great many small efforts, particularly in Africa, could be started by Mission initiative. Some of these would be single-phase projects with no further action needed. Others would be the opening gambit in a potentially much larger undertaking if the original efforts prove successful. Such projects should be identified at the start and fitted with ongoing information systems to supply baseline data and monitor any changes brought about by the intervention. This would permit an outside team of professionals from AID/Washington to judge the suitability of second-phase funding. If future funding were recommended, the Mission could renew its initial commitment, while AID/Washington prepared the paperwork necessary to justify a much larger second phase.

It is necessary under the current AID system to consider Congressional presentations and future budgeting cycles. Adopting the preceding suggestion would pose difficulties within this budgeting system. It would not be possible to schedule all second-phase projects with equal certainty since some might be terminated following the pre-implementation phase. If the Phase Two funding were sufficiently flexible to be used when the original work showed promise, or diverted to another project in the country (perhaps five small undertakings approved by the Mission in lieu of a ten million dollar second phase), the country allocations would not change, but merely the monetary allocations within the country. This could provide a workable combination of structure (a country's budget allocation) and flexibility (project funding decisions) to improve the utilization of AID funds in the field.

Careful consideration must be given to creating incentives to making a project successful, rather than the amount of funds programmed, the primary objective of AID. If authority is to be delegated to the field to start up process approach projects, appropriate incentives can be built in by giving AID/Washington responsibility for reviewing project progress, for instance, after two years have elapsed. The AID/Washington review team would have the authority to recommend termination of the project if developments did not appear promising, or to approve the project for continuation or increased funding levels if the project appeared to be on the right course.

In summary, it is recommended that, for "New Directions" projects that will use a process approach,

- The existing system of project review and approval should be restructured, rather than merely adjusted (in an attempt to improve efficiency) by delegation of greatly expanded authority to the field;

- Mission Directors' authority to get projects underway should be delineated, setting forth clear regulations for the exercise of this authority;

- Projects should be structured with information systems that permit assessments by AID/Washington, after a reasonable amount of time has elapsed, to decide on continuation or termination of each project;

- AID/Washington should strengthen its evaluation capability to carry out this recommendation; and

- AID should focus on the results of project implementation, using data from successful projects to report to Congress, rather than concentrating on a catalogue of often unfulfilled and unevaluated promises of what proposed projects might deliver to the rural poor.

Using this approach, it will be possible to assess performance of field personnel in terms of their ability to initiate projects having a reasonable chance of success. In this respect the incentives issue will be resolved in a manner that directly contributes to the development of sound projects.

NOTES

1 For further information on this point regarding the Africa Bureau, see *Project Development in East and Southern Africa*, op. cit., and Operations Appraisal Staff, Office of the Auditor General, AID, "Appraisal of Africa Programs and Operations," July 5, 1977, to be referred to as the *OAS* report.

2 AID/Washington staff point out that the appropriate handbooks assume fifteen months are needed to design a project. However, as Chapter 3 points out, delays in review should not be chargeable to design, since few design changes appear to emerge.

3 The intervals between PP submission and approval were one month for the Chile project, twenty-five days for Colombia, thirteen days for Zaire, and five days for Haiti. For further details, see the chronology at the beginning of Chapter 3.

4 The Colombia Small Farmer Development Project was categorized as "research" and did not require economic projections.

5 In a related study for AID, DAI analyzed the economic projections for irrigated riceland for five different projects

operating in the same geographic area. Each project designer managed to increase the net income and yield projections from the same hectarage, utilizing all previous designers' best estimates and adding a few innovations. The final paper projected an income increase larger by a factor of eight than did the first paper. In other projects, a diminishing marginal utility of income argument was used to bolster the projected income benefits of the projects to urban and rural poor.

[6] Another popular strategy is to approve a project conditionally, with reservations and necessary revisions.

[7] The subjects are important and should be an integral part of project design. It is the review/approval process that has corrupted the field designers' good intentions with a requirement to satisfy information requirements that are not useful to project design.

[8] PID information requirements are increasing under the new arrangements, and it remains to be seen whether this ultimately negates most of the time and cost savings of eliminating the PRP.

[9] Cable from U.S. Secretary of State to American Embassies/ Africa, March 30, 1977.

[10] Cable from E. B. Hogan, R. H. Nooter, and A. Shakow to Mission Directors, June 26, 1977 (State 231696).

[11] Cable from Mission Director, USAID/Addis Ababa to AID/Washington, 6/17/77.

[12] AID Organization Task Force Report, Preliminary Version, 1977, Section III, pp. 6-7.

[13] Some AID projects using this approach use different terminology, e.g., "pilot project -- full-fledged project approach." Obviously the concern here is with the content of the process recommended rather than the labels attached to it.

[14] There are other limitations on the appropriateness of this suggestion. Some countries have a surfeit of potential foreign aid donors and little interest in starting something small with only the possibility of it becoming a bigger project. Where the problem is one of human resources development, or expatriate assistance to a line ministry, dual-phased projects would not be suitable.

III
Principal Conclusions and Recommendations

10
Principal Conclusions and Recommendations

INTRODUCTION

The purpose of this chapter is to synthesize the findings and recommendations presented in earlier chapters. General conclusions are based not only upon the twelve cases examined in detail, but upon complementary work for AID undertaken over the last five years, exhibited in Annex B. Readers have been provided with sufficient background information to draw their own conclusions.

AID AND THE "NEW DIRECTIONS" MANDATE

The "New Directions" legislation of 1973 constituted a significant departure from the past in the sense that, for the first time, U.S. foreign assistance was to be targeted at the "poor majority," and in particular the rural poor of developing nations.

Since then Congress has become increasingly impatient to see results and has passed further legislation that seriously restricts AID's latitude in implementing the "New Directions" mandate. This brings forth the first important observation. The 1973 legislation saddled AID with an extremely complex task, and Congressional expectations have been premature and counterproductive.

There is an interesting analogy here with domestic American experience in the "War on Poverty" during the 1960s. Most participants in and observers of that effort would agree today that too much was attempted too quickly, in the sense of trying too much before a viable set of implementation strategies had been defined. Congress has now tasked AID with a similar responsibility in countries with a diversity of cultures, with political priorities that often differ from those of the United States, and with characteristically weak economic institutions.

Policy changes as drastic as those written into the 1973 legislation cannot be expected to bear fruit overnight. Even with an efficiently run bureaucracy, time is needed to develop implementation strategies; projects must be designed to reflect these strategies and time must be allowed for project implementation and for redesign of projects as evidence from the first efforts becomes available.

Although Congressional expectations have been unwarranted and AID has been constrained by legislative requirements, it must also be said that the Agency has not made the best use of the last few years in finding ways to implement the "New Directions" mandate.[1] It has not devoted sufficient resources either to develop a set of operationally useful strategies or to test them. Consequently, AID does not yet know how to meet the Congressional mandate to get the benefits of development to the poor.

These observations lead to the first recommendation:

RECOMMENDATION ONE

AID should develop and test alternative strategies to bring development benefits to the rural poor. It should monitor and evaluate these efforts. This would allow AID (were it sufficiently staffed and supported) to reach empirical conclusions on what works and what does not.

THE AID REVIEW AND APPROVAL SYSTEM

Agency Problems

While lively debate over how to implement the "New Directions" mandate is both understandable and praiseworthy, there is little to be gained from staging such debate in the midst of the review of individual project proposals. Rather than concentrating on finding ways to meet its newly defined objectives, AID has instead attempted to demonstrate to Congress that projects as proposed <u>appear</u> to be satisfying the new mandate. This has generated logjams of project paperwork, which has minimal value in terms of accomplishing developmental goals. The time and energy AID expends in project reviews reflect an understandable, if misguided, attempt to meet the unrealistic demands posed by Congress.

The most obvious manifestation of this problem is the occurrence of unconscionably long delays between submission of projects for review, and final Washington approval. For eight of the twelve projects studied, average review and approval time was ten months. For projects within the Africa and Near East Bureaus, the reasons for the delays were:

- Unclear chains of command;
- Uncertainty about procedures and requirements; and
- Arbitrary and discretionary decision criteria.

That long delays in reviewing and approving projects need not occur is obvious from the procedures established within the Latin America Bureau. There, projects are developed and monitored according to a tight schedule, packaged with an eye toward the review requirements, and approved very soon after submission of the PP.

A more serious problem is that AID/Washington has shown itself unable to improve the quality of projects utilizing a process approach during the review and approval process.[2] Projects are reviewed by a varied set of individuals, who have their own special interests to promote and protect. Among the twelve projects studied in this report, neither the rapid approval of four projects (which serious assessment could have found wanting in many respects), nor the long delays in approval of the other eight improved the quality of the design. In only one instance was a major substance change made in the field submission during the final review. In this instance, after lengthy disagreement between AID/Washington (NE/TECH) and the field, the entire design of the Afghanistan Integrated Rural Development Project was discarded, and a minor research component substituted.

Needed Agency Reform

While AID/Washington has official responsibility to ensure that the Congressional directives are carried out, the field Missions are far better placed to design projects that fulfill the intentions of the

Congress and fit host country development priorities. Because AID/Washington has proved to be unable to improve on the substance of project designs submitted from the field, continuation of its present role in review and approval is open to serious question. These observations lead to the following recommendation:

> RECOMMENDATION TWO
>
> Approval authority for projects costing up to two million dollars over a period of up to twenty-four months should be delegated to the field. Further funding should await a careful assessment by AID/Washington staff, based in part upon output from a functioning information system built into the project from its earliest stages.

Overcoming Congressional Restrictions

The ability of AID to meet the Congressional mandate has been further compromised by certain restrictions Congress itself has placed on AID operations. These restrictions involve, essentially, the requirement for detailed planning, budgeting and scheduling of development activities. When the development goal requires behavior change among the very poor, a process that must, to be successful, continue after the foreign assistance funds are exhausted, there are few certainties about appropriate technologies, optimal intervention techniques or the timing and budgeting of activities. Projects with an evolutionary component, which rely heavily on the outcome of interactions between development assistance technicians and local participants, are incompatible with Congressional restrictions. In addition, prior approval by the Congress of each proposed project removes AID's flexibility to shift development assistance as projects are more or less successful. This leads to the following recommendations:

RECOMMENDATION THREE

Section 611(a)(1) of the Foreign Assistance Act, requiring adequate planning prior to obligation of project funds, should be amended to allow project planning to proceed during implementation for those project components that are evolutionary in nature.

RECOMMENDATION FOUR

The Foreign Assistance Act should be amended to allow AID to make intracountry reallocations of approved project funds.

INCENTIVES FOR EFFECTIVE PROJECT IMPLEMENTATION

Incentives are lacking for AID's staff to concentrate on effective project implementation. Rewards come from getting projects approved and into the implementation stage.

The best Washington staff are concerned with issuing yet more directives on how projects must look before being approved. In the field, AID staff are given strong incentives to obligate funds and get projects started. After the Project Agreement is signed, the actual implementation requirements -- logistical orders, negotiations with the host country's implementing agency, generation of the implementation plan, selection and deployment of the technical assistance team -- are often left to lower-ranking staff who are not equipped either with the skills or with the authority to overcome the myriad bureaucratic roadblocks to effective implementation support.

In short, incentives within the system remain with project design and approval, all focused on AID/Washington. Implementation arrangements are given light treatment in project design; implementation support is consigned to the lower floors of overseas Missions, and evaluation is virtually nonexistent.

AID currently has no sustained capability to measure the development impact of the projects it supports, either in absolute terms or relative to the level of funds expended. It is in this domain that the Agency's capacities must be strengthened if the existing incentive system is to be effectively transformed. AID professionals will respond positively, it is argued here, to measures that create incentives for quality of project performance, as opposed to promise. The state of the art in project evaluation work is sufficiently advanced for the Agency to move toward rigorous, systematic assessments of implementation efforts and their results. With project approval authority delegated to the field, AID/Washington should meet its responsibility to the Congress by objectively evaluating field operations.

This conclusion leads to the following recommendation:

RECOMMENDATION FIVE

AID should restructure its priorities and incentives to focus on the actual implementation of development projects overseas. This calls for substituting a "development benefits delivered" incentive for the current "funds obligated" incentive. This can be accomplished in part by establishing a central office to perform cross-project evaluations of development impact. Projects initiated by Missions should be reviewed after two years by the evaluation office, and those that are not on target or do not show high promise should be terminated at that time. Implementation problems should be documented and analyzed with a view toward greatly increasing AID's knowledge of this complex and as yet ignored area of development assistance.

NOTES

1 DAI has often had occasion to examine projects attempting to reach the rural poor that were funded by other donors, including the World Bank. Our overall impression is that these donors struggle with the same problem as AID does in operationalizing their own new directions.

2 This is not to argue that AID/Washington review has not served to catch egregious errors in some project documents sub-

mitted for approval. However since the essence of the process approach is to be flexible and to respond to changing circumstances in the field, there is little that the AID/Washington review process has to offer to improve project design.

Annex A

LEGISLATIVE HISTORY OF SECTION 611(a)(1) OF THE FOREIGN ASSISTANCE ACT

The Foreign Assistance Act of 1961 amended attempts to ensure that funds are not obligated for a project until adequate planning is done and reasonable cost estimates completed.[1] Section 611 provides as follows:

> (a) No agreement or grant which constitutes an obligation of the United States Government in excess of $100,000 under Section 1311 of the Supplemental Appropriation Act, 1955, as amended (31 U.S.C. 200), shall be made for any assistance authorized under Titles I, II, and VI of Chapter 2 and Chapter 4 of Part I;
>
> (1) If such agreement or grant requires substantive technical or financial planning, until engineering, financial, and other plans necessary to carry out such assistance, and a reasonably firm estimate of the cost to the United States Government of providing such assistance, have been completed; and
>
> (2) If such agreement or grant requires legislative action within the recipient country, unless such legislative action may reasonably be anticipated to be completed in time to permit the orderly accomplishment of the purposes of such agreement or grant.
>
> (b) Plans required under subsection (a) of this section for any water or related land resource construction project or program shall include a computation of benefits and costs made insofar as practicable in accordance with the procedures set forth in the Memorandum of the President dated May 15, 1962, with respect to such computations.

(c) To the maximum extent practicable, all contracts for construction outside the United States made in connection with any agreement or grant subject to subsection (a) of this section shall be made on a competitive basis.

(d) Subsection (a) of this section shall not apply to any assistance furnished for the sole purpose of preparation of engineering, financial, and other plans.

(e) In addition to any other requirements of this section, no assistance authorized under Titles I, II, or VI of Chapter 2 or Chapter 4 of Part I of this Act shall be furnished with respect to any capital assistance project estimated to cost in excess of $1,000,000 until the head of the agency primarily responsible for administering Part I of the Act has received and taken into consideration a certification from the principal officer of such agency in the country in which the project is located as to the capability of the country (both financial and human resources) to effectively maintain and utilize the project taking into account among other things the maintenance and utilization of projects in such country previously financed or assisted by the United States.

An examination of the legislative history of Section 611(a)(1) demonstrates why Congress considered it necessary to legislate these basic principles. The source of this legislation was Section 517(a) of the Mutual Security Act introduced in 1958. The need was reflected in a report of the House Foreign Affairs Committee. It stated:[2]

> [F]unds are obligated, and consequently may be carried forward from year to year until expended, on the basis of an agreement with a foreign government even though such agreement is not supported by construction or procurement contracts. The result is that funds are appropriated by the Congress to build factories and for other projects 2 or 3 years, in a number of cases, before the engineering plans...are completed.

The committee recognizes the inevitability of delays in negotiating and planning projects with foreign governments, particularly with undeveloped governments. It fully approves the desire of our officials to proceed with caution and to delay actual expenditure of funds until all problems have been worked out. It should not be necessary, however, to appropriate funds until the process of planning, organization and taking the necessary legal and legislative action in the recipient country is further advanced than is the present practice.

It [Section 517(a)] should in the future prevent the International Cooperation Administration [the predecessor of A.I.D.] from requesting appropriation of funds or from obligating funds until our own officials and the recipient country have reached a firm decision as to what is contemplated jointly to be done: when, where, and at what cost.

* * * * * * * *

The Committee recognizes the need for careful planning for overseas projects and the inevitability of delays in negotiation and in action by foreign governments. It is not suggested that surveys, discussions and engineering work which require 3 years to complete should be rushed through in a year. This action is intended, however, to encourage the ICA to carry forward negotiations with foreign governments, to evaluate the readiness of the recipient government to put up the necessary funds, to take appropriate action for such purposes as acquiring rights of way, and to encourage both ICA and the foreign government to do sufficient planning and engineering work so as to be informed of all major problems likely to be encountered before United States funds are committed for financing any project.

* * * * * * * *

These provisions are intended to require the ICA to delay the obligation of funds

> until it has reached a decision that each project has been adequately planned and that the foreseeable obstacles which are to be encountered can be overcome."

The Chairman of the Foreign Affairs Committee described one of the ineffective ICA projects that contributed to the need for this legislation. Considerable funds had been obligated to construct a sawmill on Taiwan and no building contracts had been awarded although one of the justifications for contract services is to determine what type sawmill should be built.

The Chairman then went on to explain the purposes of the legislation as follows:

> The process of obligating funds for projects has been made a more serious step. This amendment...has been termed the most constructive proposal to come out of our committee. Obligation of funds is to be made only when preliminary studies as to feasibility have been completed and only when the preliminaries required of a recipient country are within sight of completion.... This amendment, while undoubtedly complicating the tasks of the administrators, should do much to help avert such errors in judgment as have accounted for much of the adverse publicity of the past 2 years.
>
> * * * * * * * *
>
> Under normal United States Government procedures, appropriated funds which have not been obligated lapse and are returned to the Treasury at the end of the fiscal year. Obligated funds may be carried forward. Obligations normally involve contracts with outside firms for goods to be delivered, real property to be purchased or leased, or work or services to be performed, and so forth.
>
> The ICA is permitted to obligate funds and thus to carry them forward into succeeding fiscal years on the basis of an agreement with a foreign country, that is, the ICA and the foreign country can agree that a power dam shall be constructed and the

funds for this purpose are considered obligated.

Thus, Section 611(a)(1) was the result of problems caused by the obligation of funds for a general purpose, such as a dam or a sawmill, without having specific construction plans or cost estimates.

Most of the legislative history of Section 611(a)(1) indicates that Congress was concerned with capital projects and the construction of physical facilities. However, the Executive Branch requested that Conference Committee revise proposed Section 517(a) to expressly refer only to "construction projects costing in excess of $1,000,000." In rejecting the request Congress implied that the legislation was intended to apply to the various forms of assistance provided by AID under the titles to the FAA mentioned in that Section.

The legislation was generally worded; the identification of the sort of "assistance" to be provided and the details of the plans to execute it were left to the discretion of the Executive. The threshold question, therefore, in determining the application of the legislation is: "What is the assistance being provided?"

NOTES

1 The following discussion includes excerpts from interviews with attorneys of the General Counsel's Office, from a memo from GC/AFR on "Entente Livestock II," February 20, 1976, and The Foreign Assistance Act, 1961, Amended Part III, Chapter I, General Provisions.

2 Ibid.

Annex B

DAI ACTIVITIES IN AGRICULTURE AND RURAL DEVELOPMENT

Activity Number	Subject	Beginning Date	Level of Effort in Person-Months	Report Title
1	Research: Local Action	July 1973	75	Strategies for Small Farmer Development (two volumes) Boulder, Colorado: Westview Press, 1976
2	Research: Women in Development		4	Women in Rural Development, Boulder, Colorado, Westview Press, 1976
3	Implementation: One long-term advisor for the District Development Program of the Kenya Ministry of Finance and Planning	January 1975	25	Some Issues Related to District Development District Planning: Proposals for Local Level Planning and Management Monitoring and Evaluating Rural Development Programs Lessons from the Special Rural Development Program: A Summary
4	Evaluation: AID's Project Design and Evaluation Seminar	May 1975	1.7	An Evaluation Module for AID
5	Design: Mali	June 1975	2.25	Contributions to PP: Mali Rural Development
6	Design: Liberia	August 1975	10.4	Contributions to the Joint IBRD-AID Bong County Integrated Rural Development Project Contributions to the Planning of the Bong County Integrated Rural Development Project Contributions to the Planning of the Upper Lofa County Integrated Rural Development Project
7	Design: Support to CODEL, Inc., in project development	August 1975	2.5	Hanang District Village Health Project
8	Design: Tanzania FT	September 1975	1	Contributions to PP: Agriculture Manpower Development
9	Research: Small Farmer Risk-Taking	October 1975	4	Small Farmer Risk-Taking
10	Design: Colombia	October 1975	2	Contributions to PP: Colombia Small Farmer Development
11	Design: Upper Volta	October 1975	1	Contribution to PRP: Oncho Areas Village Development Fund
12	Design: Chile	October 1975	10.5	Contributions to PP: Small Farm Management and Technology
13	Design: Haiti	October 1975	2.1	Contributions to PP: Integrated Agricultural Development
14	Design: Upper Volta OP	October 1975	6.6	Contributions to PPs: Oncho Areas Village Development Fund; Women's Roles in Development
15	Design: Guatemala	November 1975	1.2	Contribution to PP : Small Farmer Development
16	Development Strategy: Sierra Leone	November 1975	5.4	Sierra Leone Program Design
17	Design: Ghana	November 1975	2.5	Contributions to PP: District Planning/ Rural Development - Phase I

Activity Number	Subject/Title	Beginning Date	Level of Effort in Person-Months	Report Title
18	Design: Colombia Nutrition	February 1976	0.6	Contribution to PRP: Nutrition Loan
19	Design: Zaire (North Shaba)	February 1976	0.5	Contribution to PRP: North Shaba Maize Production
20	Evaluation: Egypt	February 1976	2.4	Bringing Developmental Change to Rural Egypt: A Study of the Organization for the Reconstruction and Development of the Egyptian Village
21	Design: Upper Volta	March 1976	8	Contribution to PPs (continued):. Oncho Areas Village Development Fund; Women's Roles in Development
22	Evaluation: Technoserve	March 1976	2.7	Interim Evaluation of Technoserve
23	Implementation: Three Long-term Advisors and Short Term Assistance to the National Community Development Service, Bolivia	April 1976	50	Completed
24	Research: Process Design Application in AID Projects with Tracking Through the Review and Approval Process	June 1976	35	The "New Directions Mandate": Studies in Project Design, Approval and Implementation
25	Design: Selection Criteria for Feeder Roads in Colombia	June 1976	1	Methodology and Selection Criteria for the Selection of Farm to Market Roads Under the "Pico y Pala" Program
26	Evaluation: Afghanistan	June 1976	4.5	An Evaluation of the Rural Works Program, Phase I
27	Design: Niger	June 1976	1.4	Contribution to PP: Niamey Department Development - Phase I
28	Research: Alternative Strategies for Local Organizational Development in Eight Countries	August 1976		Ongoing, fieldwork completed in Cameroon, Guatemala, North Yemen, Peru, Philippines, Upper Volta
29	Design: Zaire	August 1976	4.3	Contribution to PP: North Shaba Maize Production
30	Development Strategy: Sudan	August 1976	3.8	Strategies for the Reintroduction of Development Assistance to the Sudan
31	Evaluation: NRECA	September 1976	3.1	An Evaluation of the Impact of the National Rural Electric Cooperative Association (The Philippines, Nicaragua and Bolivia)
32	Design: Afghanistan	September 1976	8.4	Contribution to: Logar Integrated Rural Development Project, Mohammed Agha District
33	Design: Ethiopia	October 1976	3.3	Contribution to PRP: Southern Gamo Gofa Area Rehabilitation
34	Research: Information Systems	November 1976	8.75	Information for Decisionmaking in Rural Development (two volumes)
35	Design: Africa AT	November 1976	9.6	Contribution to PRP: Improved Rural Technology in Africa
36	Implementation: Ethiopia	February 1977	5.8	Completed

Activity Number	Subject/Title	Beginning Date	Level of Effort in Person-Months	Report Title
37	Implementation: Information System Design for the Hanang Primary Health Care Project (PVO), Tanzania	April 1977	2.35	Information Systems for Project Management and Evaluation in Northern Tanzania: A Case Study
38	Implementation: Philippines, Bicol	April 1977	3.5	The Bicol River Basin Development Project: Some Preliminary Observations
39	Development Strategy: Philippines, DAP	April 1977	3.4	Contribution to Revision of DAP
40	Evaluation: Haiti	May 1977	4	Evaluation of the Haiti Small Farmer Coffee Project
41	Design: Tanzania Village Development	May 1977	5.5	Contribution to PP: Arusha Planning/Village Development
42	Evaluation: Tanzania Livestock	June 1977	1	Tanzania Livestock Marketing and Development Project, Evaluation Report
43	Research: REDSO/East	June 1977	6.85	Personnel Requirements for Project Development in East and Southern Africa
44	Implementation: North Shaba Rural Development Project, Long- and Short-Term Assistance	June 1977	288	(Ongoing)
45	Development Strategy: Reorganization of AID	July 1977	0.6	Reorganizing AID to Promote Development
46	Development Strategy: USDA Contributions to Development	July 1977	0.3	Technical Assistance to Promote Agricultural and Rural Development
47	Implementation: Philippines, Bicol	August 1977	4.4	Project-Level Organizational Linkages and Integrated Rural Development
				Implementing Integrated Area Development in the Bicol: Recommendations
				Anticipating Roadblocks in Organizational Terrain: How Development Project Organization Design Makes a Difference
48	Research: FAO Information System	October 1977	2	A System for Monitoring and Evaluating FAO's Rural Development Activities
49	Evaluation: ROCAP	November 1977	2	An Evaluation of the PIADIC Project Agricultural Research and Information Systems
50	Implementation: Information System Design for the Kitui Primary Health Care Project (PVO), Kenya	November 1977	3	A Monitoring and Evaluation System for the Kitui Primary Health Care Program
51	Implementation: Long- and Short-Term Assistance to the Southern Gamo Gofa Project, Ethiopia	January 1978	3	Completion of Contract Report: Southern Gamo Gofa Area Rehabilitation Pre-Implementation Grant
52	Design: Rwanda	February 1978	1	Contribution to PP: Rwanda Rural Education Project

Activity Number	Subject/Title	Beginning Date	Level of Effort in Person-Months	Report Title
53	Research: Socioeconomic Impact Assessment of Labor-Intensive Feeder Roads in Colombia	Feburary 1978	4.9	An Information Research Project on the Impact of Labor-Intensive Feeder Roads in Colombia: A Case Study
54	Design: Gamo Gofa, Ethiopia	March 1978	2.1	Contribution to PP: Southern Gamo Gofa Area Rehabilitation Project
55	Evaluation: Bangladesh	March 1978	1.3	Contribution to: Evaluation of Food for Relief Work Program
56	Design: Sudan	March 1978	6.8	Contribution to PP: Southern Manpower Development
57	Implementation: Jamaica Integrated Area Development Project	April 1978	7.0	Extension Training Program for the Jamaica Integrated Rural Development Project Integrated Rural Development Project Farm Plan Crop Production Costing Handbook Farm Planning Handbook for Field Officers
58	Evaluation: Impact Study (PVO)	May 1978	9.2	Final Report: The Development Impact of Private Voluntary Organizations: Kenya and Niger
59	Implementation: Philippines, Bicol River Basin Development Program	June 1978	3.5	Organization Design and Implementation in Selected Bicol Projects: Progress Report #1 Basic Steps in Critical Path Analysis: Network Modelling and Float Calculation for Project Implementation Supervising Agricultural Extension: Cases and Guidelines for Field Supervisors and Project Designers Organization Design and Implementation in Selected Bicol Projects, Progress Report #2 Farmer Organization for Irrigation Water Management
60	Design: Peru	June 1978	.8	Assistance in Preparation of PIDs on Small Farmer Organization and Rural Public Works Projects
61	Implementation: Long- and Short-Term Assistance to Indonesia PDP I	June 1978	182.0	(Ongoing)
62	Research: Rural Development Project Design; FAO Investment Centre, Rome	August 1978	3	Designing Rural Development Projects: An Approach
63	Design: Sudan	September 1978	4	Contribution to PIDs: Agriculture Sector Support; Health Sector Support; and Rural Infrastructure (Southern Region)

Activity Number	Subject/Title	Beginning Date	Level of Effort in Person-Months	Report Title
64	Implementation: Research and Consulting on the Administration and Organization of Integrated Rural Development Projects	September 1978	254.0	(Ongoing)
65	Evaluation: Zaire	September 1978	.8	No written report
66	Evaluation: Cameroon	October 1978	2.5	Evaluation of North Cameroon Seed Multiplication Project (also in French)
67	Design: Agricultural Sector Survey, Botswana	March 1979	12.0	(Ongoing)
68	Evaluation: Entente Fund Development Projects	March 1979	24.0	(Ongoing)

www.ingramcontent.com/pod-product-compliance
Lightning Source LLC
LaVergne TN
LVHW011122300926
849160LV00008B/473
9780367167776